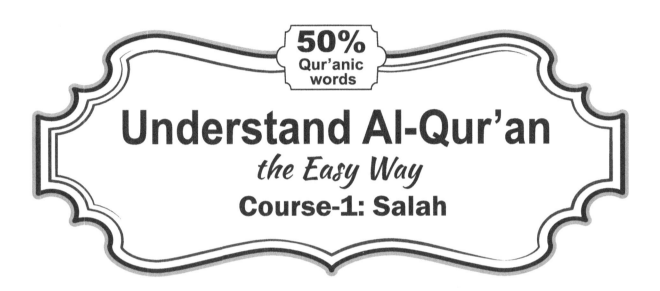

50%
Qur'anic
words

Understand Al-Qur'an
the Easy Way
Course-1: Salah

Through Surah Al-Fatihah, last **6** Surah, Azkar of Salah and Basic Arabic grammar, you will learn **232** important words that occur in the Qur'an **41,000** times (from a total of **78,000** words in the Qur'an, i.e., **50%** words of the Qur'an).

By Dr. Abdulazeez Abdulraheem

Founder & Director, Understand Al-Qur'an Academy

www.understandquran.com

Visit URL below To Get
Free Access to Understand Quran
Video Course

www.alihuda.com/programs/understand-quran-50

Book Name:

Understand Al-Qur'an *the easy way*
(Through Salah)

Course - 1

Compiled by:

Dr. Abdulazeez Abdulraheem
Founder & Director: Understand Al-Qur'an Academy

Eight Edition:

January 2020, 3000 Copies

Pages:

128

Publisher

EduSuite
Solutions Private Limited

Plot No. 13-6-434/B/41, 2nd Floor, Omnagar,
Langar House, Hyderabad - 500 008.
Telangana - INDIA
Ph.: +91- 9652 430 971 /+91-40-23511371
Website: www.understandquran.com
Email: info@understandquran.com

Research & Development

Mohsin Siddiqui
Mohammed Furqan Falahi
Aamir Irshad Faizi, Abdul Quddoos Umari
Irshad Alam Nadwi
Abdurrab Khurram Quraishi
Dr. Zarish Tabassum Mominati
Usama Saleha

Advisors

Khursheed Anwar Nadwi
Fazil Darul Uloom Nadwatul Ulama
Kamil Jamia Nizamia

Contributes

Dr. Abdul Qadir Fazlani
Khawja Nizamuddin Ahsan
Abdul Raheem Nayeem Uddin
Mohammad Younus Jamaei

Translators

Mujahidullah Khan

Arabic Font Designers

Late Shakeel Ahmad, Ayesha Fawzia

Graphic Designers

Kafeel Ahmad Faizi

Qur'anic Words Count

Tarique Azeez, Mujtaba Shareef
corpus.quran.com

Table of Contents

IMPORTANT GUIDELINES

Some guidelines for using this course effectively:

- You should be able to read Arabic text of the Qur'an to be able to use this course.
- This is a thoroughly interactive course, therefore, practice what you hear and study.
- There is no problem even if you commit mistakes. Nobody learns without first committing mistakes.
- The one who practices more will learn more even if he/she commits mistakes.
- **Remember the golden rule:**

  I listen, I forget. I see, I remember. I practice, I learn. I teach, I master.

- Remember the 3 levels of learning:
  1. Listening without paying attention. You hear only noises.
  2. Listening carelessly or with doubt. Shaitaan may create doubts about your ability to learn!
  3. Listening interactively; listening with HEART; responding immediately to the points.
- Each lesson is followed by Grammar. Grammar contents are not directly related to the main lesson because the course will become complicated and may require separate Grammar teaching before we start studying Surahs. Grammar sections build up your Arabic Grammar in parallel to the vocabulary that you learn in the main lesson. After a few lessons, you will be able to see the benefit of learning Grammar while studying the Surahs or Adhkaar.

Simple homework to master this course:

Two for Tilawat:
1. At least FIVE minutes recitation of the Qur'an from the Mushaf.
2. At least FIVE minutes recitation of the Qur'an from memory during walking, cooking, etc.

Two for Study:
1. At least TEN minutes study of this book, for the beginners.
2. 30 seconds for the study of the vocabulary booklet or sheet, preferably before or after every Salah or at any other suitable interval. Give a pledge to Allah that you will always carry the vocabulary booklet with you until you complete the course.

Two for Listening and talking to others:
1. Listening to an mp3 file or tape which contains these recitations with word-for-word meanings. You can listen to it in your car while driving and at your home while performing household chores. You can also record the contents of this course yourself and listen to it again and again.
2. Talking to your family members, friends, or colleagues for at least one minute every day about the lesson that you have learnt.

The last one for using it:
1. Recitation of the last 10 Surahs in the rotation in the Sunan and Nawafil of daily Salah. This will increase your focus in Salah and make it more enjoyable in addition to revising the meanings of different verses.

Don't forget the two supplications:
(i) For yourself رَبِّ زِدْنِي عِلْمًا; and
(ii) For your friends, "May Allah help us and them in learning the Qur'an."

The best way to learn is to teach, and the best way to teach someone is to turn him into a teacher.

UNDERSTAND AL-QUR'AN ACADEMY
www.understandquran.com

OBJECTIVES OF THE ACADEMY:

(1) To bring the Muslims back to the Qur'an and to help in bringing up a Qur'anic generation who recites the Qur'an, understands it, practices it, and conveys it to others. (2) To present Qur'an as the most interesting, easy, simple, effective, and relevant book in our daily life as well as the most important book for success in this world and the Hereafter. (3) To provide the basic knowledge of Hadith with the purpose of creating love and respect towards the Prophet Muhammad ﷺ. (4) To teach them how to read the Qur'an with Tajweed and to understand it (5) To produce the required course materials (books, videos, posters, vocabulary cards, booklets, etc.) under the supervision of Islamic scholars and design a syllabus that caters to the need of schools and Madrasah. (6) To conduct short courses for busy people or businessmen. (7) To make learning of the Qur'an easy by using easy, modern and scientific methods and techniques of teaching.

Our objective is not to produce scholars of the Qur'an. Alhamdulillah, many institutions are already doing this work. The mission of the academy is to make ordinary Muslims and school students (especially our young generation) understand the basic message of the Qur'an.

WHY THIS WORK?

Majority of the non-Arab Muslims do not understand the Qur'an. In the present scenario, the teaching of the Qur'an is extremely necessary because on the one hand there is a storm of obscenity and materialism on TV, press, and social media and on the other hand there are continuous attacks on Islam, the Qur'an, and the Prophe ﷺ to weaken our faith in the Qur'an and Islam. It is, therefore, a must for our coming generation to understand the Qur'an and the Islamic teachings to counter the challenges and to convey the true message of Allah to the world and in turn make their lives successful in this world and in the Hereafter.

BRIEF HISTORY:

By the Grace of Allah www.understandquran.com was launched in 1998. Since then we are constantly striving to make learning of the Qur'an simple, easy and effective by developing courses and related materials. Our level 1 course on understanding the Qur'an (50% of the Qur'anic words) is being taught in almost 25 countries and is translated in 20 international languages. It is relayed on five national and international TV channels too. The syllabus of Read Al-Qur'an and Understand Al-Qur'an is now implemented in more than 2000 schools, Alhamdulillah.

OUR MESSAGE

The Messenger of Allah said: بَلِّغُوا عَنِّيْ وَلَوْ اٰيَةً "Convey from me, even if it is only one verse". Therefore come and join us to spread this noble work, wherever you are; try to learn this course and introduce it in your nearby mosques, schools, Madaaris and community centers etc. Connect the children and elders to this course and build a strong team to carry out this noble task.

Lastly, we pray to Allah to accept our endeavors to serve this Magnificent Book, keep us away from show off, save us from sins, and protect us from mistakes.

رَبَّنَا تَقَبَّلْ مِنَّا اِنَّكَ اَنْتَ السَّمِيْعُ الْعَلِيْمِ، وَتُبْ عَلَيْنَا اِنَّكَ اَنْتَ التَّوَّابُ الرَّحِيْمِ، وَاغْفِرْ لَنَا، اِنَّكَ اَنْتَ الْغَفُوْرُ الرَّحِيْمِ -وَجَزَاكُمُ اللهُ خَيْرًا -

PREFACE

All Praise be to Allah, and peace and blessings be upon His Messenger, Muhammad ﷺ.

The Prophet ﷺ said: "The best of you is the one who learns the Qur'an and teaches it (to others)". In spite of this exhortation by the Prophet ﷺ, today the situation of Non-Arab Muslims is that; almost 90% of them do not understand even a single page of the Qur'an. InshaAllah, this course will help them learn the common recitations of Salah as well as the fundamentals of Arabic Grammar that will be of great help in understanding the Qur'an.

One of the most distinguishing features of this course is that it is based on common recitations instead of selections that are rarely used in everyday life. It is but natural to start the teaching of Arabic using them. There are several advantages to this approach:

- A Muslim repeats almost 150 to 200 Arabic words or around 50 sentences everyday in Salah. By understanding these sentences, he/she will be able to familiarize himself/herself with the structure of the Arabic language without any special effort.
- He/she will have a golden chance to practice it daily by talking to Allah!
- He/she will start realizing the benefits from the first lesson itself.
- He/she can immediately feel the improvement in his/her Salah in terms of attention, concentration, and attachment with Allah.

Another important feature of this course is the way the Arabic Grammar is taught. Since the purpose of this course is to help them understand the Qur'an through translation, more attention is given in this course on "Tasreef" (word construction from a root). A new simple yet powerful technique of TPI (Total Physical Interaction) is introduced to teach different forms of verbs, nouns, and pronouns. Please note that this is an introductory course and you can surely read advanced books on Arabic Grammar at a later stage.

By the end of this course, you will learn 232 words approximately. Out of them, 125 words occur in the Qur'an almost 38,300 times, i.e., almost 50% of the Qur'anic words. This does not mean that you will be able to understand 50% of the Qur'an because you may still have new words in almost every verse. However, the understanding of the Qur'an will become extremely easy after this course.

InshaAllah, you will find this course easy, interesting, and effective in terms of learning. May Allah accept our humble efforts. We request you to introduce this course in every Masjid, school, madrassah, organization, locality, and family that you know so that a trend is introduced in this Ummah to understand the Salah as well as the Qur'an.

Please note that the brackets "( )" in the translation indicate the added words for better understanding. The square brackets "[ ]" in the translation are used for those words which are there in Arabic but are not translated into English. They are also used for showing references from the Qur'an or Hadith.

May Allah forgive our mistakes. Please let us know if you find any, so that our future editions are free from them.

Abdulazeez Abdulraheem
(info@understandquran.com)
January 2020.

Quran
&
Hadith

Lesson 1a — **INTRODUCTION & Ta'awwuz**

After completing this lesson (a & b), you will learn **12 new** words, which occur **7,248** times in the Qur'an.

Study & Ponder / Propagate / Ask / Visualize Feel / Plan (Check with Scholars) / Evaluate

OBJECTIVES OF THIS COURSE:

1. To convince you that the Qur'an is easy to understand
2. To teach how to understand the Qur'an – the easy way, using word-for-word study.
3. To help you pray Salah effectively with Khushoo, i.e, humility (by teaching you 7 Surahs and Adhkaar of Salah) so that the effects of Salah are reflected in your daily lives
4. To teach how to bring the Qur'an into our lives
5. To teach basic Arabic Grammar using TPI and spoken Arabic
6. To teach 100 sentences of (Qur'an-centric) Spoken Arabic

Qur'an is easy to understand:

Allah says: « وَلَقَدْ يَسَّرْنَا الْقُرْآنَ لِلذِّكْرِ » And We have indeed made the Qur'an easy to understand and remember ». To say that Qur'an is difficult is a satanic trick. Can we be among those who negate Qur'an. Astaghfirullah.

The Book of the Qur'an is called Mushaf. Hafizi Mushaf (which is generally used for memorization of the Qur'an) usually has 600 pages. Each page has 15 lines and approximately 9 words appear in each line. This means every page has 135 words. To simplify, if we consider 130 words per page, then the Qur'an has 130x600 words, i.e., approximately 78,000 words.

If we take surahs and Adhkaar recited in a typical Salah, i.e., سُورَةُ الْفَاتِحَةِ, سُورَةُ الْفَلَقِ، سُورَةُ الْإِخْلَاصِ the last six Surahs (سُورَةُ الْكَافِرُونَ، سُورَةُ النَّصْرِ، سُورَةُ الْعَصْرِ، سُورَةُ النَّاسِ), Adhkaar of Salah (Du'aa after Adhaan and Wudoo, Tasbeehat of Rukoo' and Sajdah, Tashahud, Durood and two important Du'aas) and learn few Arabic Grammar rules then InshaAllah, we can learn 232 important words that occur 41,000 times in the Qur'an, i.e., more than 50% words of the Qur'an. Every second word that occurs in Qur'an is from Adhkaar of Salah!!!

The above are the contens of this Course which can InshaAllah be learnt in 20 hours. Isn't the Qur'an easy to understand?

Unique approach of this course:

We don't start with dry lessons such as هٰذَا بَيْتٌ كَبِيْرٌ. When are you going to repeat هٰذَا بَيْتٌ كَبِيْر؟ Perhaps if you have an Arab neighbor and his toddler comes to you crying; you take him in your lap and to console him, you say: هٰذَا بَيْتٌ كَبِيْر. That may never happen!

Our lessons start with Al-Fatihah! Talk to Allah 25 to 30 times everyday. Practice Arabic language with Allah! What an amazing start! And right on the target!

We spend almost an hour for 5 prayers talking to Allah in Arabic! Why not start from there! It is the most common sense approach and it is valid for every Muslim man, woman, old, and young, and even for a child.

We can improve our Salah:

Salah can be improved by the following:

- Try to recite slow. We don't want anyone to talk to us at very high speed; let us not therefore talk to Allah very fast.

- Concentrate on the words that you say in Salah. We don't accept anyone talking to us while his mind is somewhere else; let us then not do the same to Allah.
- Recite with feelings and emotions. We don't like to sit even for a minute with a person who talks to us like a robot.

To avoid whispering of Shaitaan in Salah, make sure that we keep all of our brain channels busy. Along with recitation, we should try to focus on Tajweed, translation, message, visualization, and recite with feelings.

Ta'awwuz:

We should recite اَعُوْذُ بِاللهِ مِنَ الشَّيْطٰنِ الرَّجِيْمِ before reciting Surah Fatihah or Qur'an. Let us first learn its translation.

Below is the format of the translation in this course. Arabic text is given in the first row. The second row contains a word-for-word translation. This is followed by the explanation of the words in the third row. Recite the complete Arabic text first, then read each word alongwith its translation and at the end read the translation of the complete text.

6 الرَّجِيْمِ.	88 2471 مِنَ الشَّيْطٰنِ	2,550 بِاللهِ	7 اَعُوْذُ
the outcast.	from Satan,	in Allah	I seek refuge
Do you think Shaitaan is close to Allah's mercy? He is rejected; outcast; thrown away from Allah's mercy. Remember the context to memorize the meanings.	from مِنْ More than 3000 times in the Qur'an	اللهِ / Allah — بِ / in	Safety first ; 'Buckle up ;' Get protection.

➢ We know Allah is above the heavens but He is very close to us. He even knows what we think. Recite the above with firm belief that Allah is responding to our request.

➢ Who is Shaitaan? Our biggest and most dangerous enemy. He has huge experience of making people slip from the time of Adam A. He made even Adam A slip in Jannah. None of us can be smarter than Adam A in resisting Shaitaan. Shaitaan has told Allah that he will attack us from the right, the left, the front, and the back.

➢ We cannot see Shaitaan, nor hit him, nor convince him to become good. The only solution and the most powerful solution is to recite اَعُوْذُ بِاللهِ.

➢ Shaitaan disobeyed Allah and was thrown away from Allah's mercy. This *Rajeem* wants us to follow him and become like him. He is there to take us to the hellfire. Therefore, feel the insecurity caused by the attacks of Shaitaan and ask Allah for protection the way a desperate beggar asks for food.

➢ Each one of us has a Shaitaan with him/her and he is continuously attacking us in our home, office, market, while we are alone or with mobile or with friends. We are in a state of continuous war with him.

➢ **1st Habit:** "Safety First;" run to Allah for protection. This is the habit of a successful person in this war against Shaitaan. This is the First of the 12 habits that we will learn in Surah Al-Fatihah.

Lesson 2a | **Surah Al-Fatihah (1-3)**

After completing this lesson 2 (a & b), you will learn **27 new** words, which occur **8,638** times in the Qur'an.

Introduction: Surah Al-Fatihah is the first complete Surah of the Qur'an. It is so important that we asked to recite it every day, in every Salah, and in every Raka'ah! In this lesson, we will take first three verses of the Surah.

	115		57		39
	الرَّحِيْمِ ①		الرَّحْمٰنِ	اللهِ	بِسْمِ
the Most Merciful.		**the Most Gracious,**		**(of) Allah,**	**In the name**
Words of this type show continuity. Beautiful جَمِيْل Good mannered كَرِيْم ²⁷ Continually Merciful اَلرَّحِيْم		Words of this type show intensity. Extremely angry غَضْبٰن Intensely Merciful رَحْمٰن			اِسْم ب name in أَسْمَاء ⁺: names

> **Second Habit:** Say Bismillah before you start or do anything like eating, sleeping, reading, writing etc. Be confident and hopeful that Ar-Rahmaan is always with you. He will definitely help you.

> The more we ponder upon and believe in the attributes of Allah the more we will feel the power and effect of reciting Bismillah.

> رَحْمٰن means extremely merciful. رَحِيْم means continuously merciful. Allah is Rahman as well as Raheem, i.e., He is blessing us with a heavy and continuous rain of mercy.

> Don't forget Allah at happy occasions. Have good opinion and hope in Allah at the time of trial. Just say, my Rabb has always blessed me extensively and definitely there is something good for me in this trial.

> **Third Habit:** Always have positive thinking about Allah, i.e., think positive about Allah because He is اَلرَّحْمٰن and اَلرَّحِيْم . He takes care of us and fulfills all our needs with love and kindness. He has created us and given us eyes, ears, brain, hands and feet. He blessed us with parents, relatives, and friends. He has made all arrangements for our comfortable living.

> There are many benefits of having positive thoughts about Allah, like peaceful life, happiness, success, health, tranquility, satisfaction, better relationships, etc. This is million times better than the modern concept of mere positive thinking.

	73	199		149	43
	الْعٰلَمِيْنَ ②	رَبِّ		لِلهِ	اَلْحَمْدُ
of the worlds.		**the Lord**	**(are) for Allah**		**All praise and thanks**
world عَالَم worlds ⁺ عَالَمِيْن Imagine billions of people; trillions of insects; zillions of galaxies		Takes care of us & helps us grow. Every cell of billions of cells.	اللهِ ل Allah for be to Allah		Two meanings of حَمْد: All Praise and thanks

> Hamd means Praise: Praise Allah with your heart. O Allah! You are the Greatest, You are the Best Creator, You are the Most Caring and Kind, etc.

> Second meaning of Hamd is to thank: Thank Him for the countless blessings. He gave you the safety, the food that you eat, and the chance to offer Salah, the chance to ask Him, etc.

- **Imagine and feel** Allah's Greatness. He is our Rabb. He takes care of all His billions of creatures and makes arrangements for their sustenance.
- **Habit No. 4:** Seek intensive knowledge and ponder upon the Universe. A serious study of science, mathematics and history will make you realize How Great is our Rabb, the creator and sustainer of the Universe. This way, you will praise Him from the depth of your heart.
- **Evaluate:** How many times did I get influenced by this world and forget to say اَلْحَمْدُ لِلّٰهِ ?
- **Habit No. 5:** Thank Allah in every moment and in any situation whether you are eating, drinking, travelling, sleeping, waking up or getting blessings at different occasions.

الرَّحِيْمِ ③	الرَّحْمٰنِ
the Most Merciful	**The Most Gracious,**

- Rahmah means to take care of someone with extreme care and love, and his/her needs. See how Allah is continuously showering His mercy on us. Just take one example. To change the weather, Allah is making earth to rotate around the Sun at the whopping speed of 20 kilometers per second. We don't even feel a small jerk. Allah is controlling it otherwise the earthquakes would have tuned our earth to dust and debris.
- The Prophet ﷺ said: "He who does not show mercy to others will not be shown mercy (by Allah)." [Bukhari]. Therefore be merciful to others on this day, this time or after this Salah in which you heard or read this verse. Take care of them with love. This is the **Habit No. 6.**

Lesson 3a Surah Al-Fatihah (4-5)

After completing this lesson 3 (a & b), you will learn **33 new** words, which occur **12,089** times in the Qur'an.

Introduction: In this lesson, we will study verses 4 and 5 of Surah Al-Fatihah.

اَعُوْذُ بِاللهِ مِنَ الشَّيْطٰنِ الرَّجِيْمِ ۞ بِسْمِ اللهِ الرَّحْمٰنِ الرَّحِيْمِ ۞

الدِّيْنِ ۗ ④ 92	يَوْمِ 405	مٰلِكِ 3
(of) Judgment.	**(of) the day**	**Master**
Deen has two meanings: ❶ Day of Judgment, the day of results for our good; ❷ System of life (Islam)	يَوْمُ الْجُمُعَة، يَوْمُ الْقِيَامَة، يَوْمُ الْعِيد Days + أَيَّام	مٰلِك: master (مَلَائِكَة +)مَلَك:angel

On the Day of Judgment Allah will have the sole authority; nobody shall have any power. He alone will judge among the people.

➤ On that day no one can intercede except the one who is given the permission by Allah.

➤ Day of Judgment will be a terrible day. Man will run away from his brother, his mother, his father, his wife, and his son. Everyone will be worried about himself or herself.

➤ While reading this Ayah we should anticipate Allah's mercy that He will reward us for our good deeds. Simultaneously we should fear the punishment for our wrongdoings.

➤ He made us Muslims without our asking; just out of His mercy. Now that we are asking Him for Jannah, we hope that He will grant us our Du'aa.

➤ **Habit No. 7:** Plan for everyday keeping Aakhirah in front of you. Remember the death, the grave, the resurrection, and the judgment day. Pray Salah on time and don't miss Tilawah and Adhkaar. Keep healthy and make sure to not use eyes, ears, tongue, hands, and feet in wrongdoings. Use your life, your youth, your money, and knowledge the right way.

نَسْتَعِيْنُ ۗ ⑤ 1	وَاِيَّاكَ	نَعْبُدُ	اِيَّاكَ 24
We ask for help.	**and You alone**	**we worship**	**You alone**
To worship or to do anything, we need Allah's help.	وَ : and In this context also, اِيَّاكَ means **You alone**.	This word is from عِبَادَة:worship	In this context only اِيَّاكَ means **You alone**. اِيَّا does not mean alone!

➤ Allah has created us so that we worship Him. He said: I have not created the Jinns and the humans except that they worship Me (Surah Al-Zariyat, 56).

➤ Ibadah actually means not only to worship but also to obey Allah's orders, to refrain from disobeying Him, to offer Salah, to fast, to give alms, to go for Hajj, to invite others towards Islam, to seek knowledge and Halal earning, to serve others, etc. All these are acts of Ibadah.

➤ Among these, Salah is the most important Ibadah. Whoever leaves Salah intentionally he commits Kufr and demolishes an important pillar of Islam.

➤ Ask: O Allah! Help me to worship You in the best way, in the way that pleases You.

➤ **Habit No. 8:** We should have *Niyyah* (intention) of Ibadah for every good task. Real peace of mind and true success can be achieved by Ibadah only. We are made up of body and soul. If the soul is not 'fed' with worshipping Allah, we can never be happy. Look at so many musicians and movie starts who take drugs or even committed suicide because Ibadah is missing in their life.

➤ وَإِيَّاكَ نَسْتَعِينُ: Without the help of Allah we cannot quench our thirst, then how can we worship Him without His help? Therefore, recite this Ayah with this feeling: O Allah! I beg for Your help in this Salah and in doing every task after this Salah. Please help me whenever I am in trouble.

➤ People hate you if you ask them for help but Allah loves that we ask Him; again and again; and for everything! He loves to accept the Du'aas. The Prophet ﷺ said: Du'aa is the worship!

➤ **Habit No. 9:** Ask for Allah's help in everything. How? The way Muhammad ﷺ and other Prophets asked! Their Du'aas are described in the Qur'an and in Ahadeeth.

<u>**An Important Suggestion:**</u>

Try to remember this Hadith Qudsi every time you recite Al-Fatihah in Salah. It will increase your focus in Salah. The Prophet ﷺ said that Allah said: I have divided the Salah between Me and My slave. Half is for Me and half for him and I give him what he asks for.

- When the slave says: اَلْحَمْدُ لِلّٰهِ رَبِّ الْعٰلَمِينَ ② then Allah says: "حَمِدَنِيْ عَبْدِيْ" which means: My slave has praised me, and

- When he says: الرَّحْمٰنِ الرَّحِيْمِ ③ then Allah says: "أَثْنٰى عَلَيَّ عَبْدِيْ" which means: My slave has lauded Me; and

- When he says: مٰلِكِ يَوْمِ الدِّيْنِ ④, then Allah says: "مَجَّدَنِيْ عَبْدِيْ" which means: My slave has glorified Me; and

- When he says: إِيَّاكَ نَعْبُدُ وَإِيَّاكَ نَسْتَعِينُ ⑤ then Allah says: This is between Me and My slave and whatever he asks for, I will provide him; and

- When he says: اِهْدِنَا الصِّرَاطَ الْمُسْتَقِيْمَ ⑥ صِرَاطَ الَّذِيْنَ اَنْعَمْتَ عَلَيْهِمْ غَيْرِ الْمَغْضُوْبِ عَلَيْهِمْ وَلَا الضَّآلِّيْنَ ⑦ then Allah says: This is for my slave and whatever he asks for, he will be provided with it. [Muslim]

Lesson 4a — Surah Al-Fatihah (6-7)

After completing this lesson (a & b), you will learn **44 new** words, which occur **15,387** times in the Qur'an.

Introduction: In this lesson, we will study verses 6 and 7 of Surah Al-Fatihah.

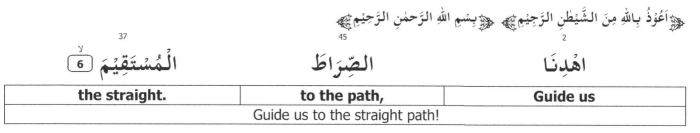

اَعُوْذُ بِاللهِ مِنَ الشَّيْطٰنِ الرَّجِيْمِ ۞ بِسْمِ اللهِ الرَّحْمٰنِ الرَّحِيْمِ ۞

المُسْتَقِيْمَ 6	الصِّرَاطَ	اهْدِنَا
the straight.	to the path,	Guide us
Guide us to the straight path!		

- "Guide us to the straight path" means show and guide us the right way in every aspect of our life.
- Becoming a Muslim is the first step of the guidance. We need Allah's guidance in performing Salah, after Salah, during work, at home, in the office or class room, while interacting with friends, in the market, at the instigation of Shaitaan, and while looking or facing anyone. So we must continuously ask for Allah's guidance.
- Source of Guidance is the Qur'an and the Sunnah (sayings and teachings of Prophet Muhammad ﷺ). Therefore, we need to understand the Qur'an as well as Ahadeeth.
- The verses of the Qur'an that are recited in the Salah, are a piece of guidance from Allah at that time. We must try to understand them. If not, then are we sincere in asking for guidance in our Salah? Every Salah is a reminder that understanding the Qur'an is not only a necessity but also an emergency!
- Allah helps us get the guidance from the Qur'an, Hadith, and from different signs in the universe if we keep reviving our faith by being regular for Salah, Tilawah, studying Seerah, staying with pious people, and staying away from Shirk, bid'ah, and evil thoughts and deeds.
- **Habit No. 10:** Ask for Allah's guidance for knowing and following the right path.

عَلَيْهِمْ	أَنْعَمْتَ	الَّذِيْنَ	صِرَاطَ
on them;	You (have) bestowed favors	(of) those	(The) path
هِمْ them | عَلَى on	favor إِنْعَام	1080 times in the Qur'an	الصِّرَاطَ المُسْتَقِيْمَ straight path

- Allah favored Prophets, truthful people, martyrs, and righteous people. Let us know what was their path in order to recite this Du'aa with understanding. Let us take the example of our beloved Prophet Muhammad ﷺ. It consisted of mainly these four tasks:
  1. Actions: Actions of heart such as belief, sincerity, love for Allah and His fear alone. Physical actions such as Salah, fasting, charity, Zakah, and Hajj, alms and good attitude and behavior etc.;
  2. Da'wah or inviting others towards Islam;
  3. Tazkiyah, i.e., Purification of people's beliefs, and actions. Purification of bad things and enforcement of good ones. The Qur'an is full of such examples.
  4. Implementing Islam in our families and in the Muslim society, ordering good and prohibiting evil to the extent possible, using the best ways of Dawah.
- If we want to be among the favored people then we must do the above four things to the extent possible.
- **Habit No. 11:** Always follow good models. Read about them, check your deeds keeping in mind their example, make a plan to act like them and try to implement it.

غَيۡرِ	الۡمَغۡضُوۡبِ	عَلَيۡهِمۡ	وَلَا	الضَّآلِّيۡنَ ٧
not	**(of) those who earned (Your) wrath**	**on them**	**and nor**	**(of) those who go astray.**

| not;
other than. | مَظۡلُوۡم : One who is wronged or oppressed

مَغۡضُوۡب : One who received the wrath | عَلَى on | هِمۡ them | هِمۡ them | وَ and | لَا not | ضَالّ : the one who goes astray

ضَالُّوۡنَ، ضَالِّيۡنَ are plural forms.
(you make plural by adding ون, ين) |

First Group (those who earned wrath):

➤ Those who know but do not act upon earn the wrath of Allah. Just imagine their terrible end in this world and in the hereafter. May Allah save us from becoming like them.

➤ Most of us want to follow a hero or a leader. So they imitate them the way they talk, wear clothes in their style and even walk like them. We must first check if these heroes or leaders are following the teachings of the Qur'an and Hadith.

Second Group (those who go astray):

➤ Those who don't know and/or don't want to know. They act without knowing the truth. They don't bother about the purpose of their creation and life. They do not try and spend time to seek the true knowledge.

➤ Let us not be among those who are lost even after having the Qur'an with us. Are we away from the Qur'an only because we do not know the Arabic language? Ask Allah to give us Tawfeeq to learn and understand the Qur'an. Make a plan for it and invest time. Resolve today that we shall not abandon learning these lessons of the Qur'anic Arabic.

Habit No. 12: Keep away from the "bad models". May Allah save us from following them.

Introduction: In this lesson, we will study the words and message of Adhaan.

اَللّٰهُ أَكْبَرُ اَللّٰهُ أَكْبَرُ   اَللّٰهُ أَكْبَرُ اَللّٰهُ أَكْبَرُ

Allah is the Greatest	Allah is the Greatest

◁ 39 كَبِيرٌ (great)   23 أَكْبَرُ (greatest)

◁ صَغِيرٌ (small)   أَصْغَرُ (smallest)

◁ 63 كَثِيرٌ (more)   88 أَكْثَرُ (most)

➢ Allah can't be compared with anyone because He is the Creator and the rest are His creations!

➢ Allah is the Greatest in power, majesty, glory, kindness and all other good attributes.

➢ Study of our own creation, the signs within us, around us such as the earth, the moon, the sun, the stars, the galaxies, etc. can help us realize Allah's greatness to some extent.

➢ The more you realize Allah's greatness the more you can praise Allah from depth of heart. You will say: O Allah! How great and magnificent are You! You will comprehend that Allah is far greater than our imagination.

➢ At the call of Fajr Salah, if I hear the call and still keep sleeping, whom did I obey? Whom did I accept as the greatest? Allah or my desires? In a similar way, you can check other things too.

➢ O Allah! Guide me to accept You as the greatest in my life. In other words, help me obey You instead of my desires, family, false leaders, or traditions. In the light of this du'aa, we must evaluate our past and draw a plan for the future.

(2 times) إِلَّا اللّٰهُ   إِلٰهَ   لَّا   571 أَنْ   1 أَشْهَدُ

except Allah	god	(there is) no	That	I bear witness
	Gods + الْهَة	مَا: no, what		

The word إِلٰه has different meanings: (1) the one who is worshipped; (2) the one who fulfills our needs; and (3) the one who is obeyed. There is no God other than Allah in all the three meanings.

I bear witness means that my talks and my actions, in my house or outside, at my office or in market, show that I:

➢ Love Allah more than anyone else.

➢ Accept Allah as my Creator, Master, Sustainer, Cherisher, and the Ruler of the entire universe. I worship and obey Him alone in all matters of my life. I seek His help alone and trust Him alone.

➢ I follow and obey His orders in all matters of my life and not my desires or others' directions.

➢ In the Qur'an, Allah ordered us to be a witness over the people, i.e., explain to them what is Islam and who is Prophet Muhammad ﷺ. This task is very important and therefore we are reminded to carry out this task in every Adhaan and Iqamah . Alas! Despite these repeated reminders we are not paying due attention to this. Let us ask Allah that He gives us Tawfeeq to be a true witness of Islam, i.e., be good callers of Islam.

(2 times) رَسُوْلُ اللّٰهِ   4 مُحَمَّدًا   أَنَّ   359 أَشْهَدُ   332

is the Messenger of Allah.	Muhammad ﷺ	That	I bear witness
رَسُوْل: messenger رُسُل: messengers	مُحَمَّد: one who is praised a lot	أَنْ: that; أَنَّ: that	

I bear witness means that my talks and my actions, in the house or outside, at the office or in market, show that:

- I love Allah and His messenger ﷺ more than anyone else;
- I accept and obey the teachings of the prophet ﷺ without questioning. I consider the Qur'an and the Sunnah as the criterion between right and wrong;
- I don't need any other evidence to follow the teachings of the Prophet ﷺ. My likes and dislikes are guided by the Prophet's likes and dislikes.

Come to	the Salah.	Come to	the prosperity
حَيَّ عَلَى	الصَّلَوٰةِ (2 times)	حَيَّ عَلَى	الْفَلَاحِ (2 times)

- The words are "Come to Salah" and not "Offer Salah wherever you are," i.e., come to Masjid. The Qur'an asks us to establish Salah by praying it with Imam and other Muslims in Jama'ah.
- If we establish Salah, then Allah will give us all types of success and prosperity. Some of them are:
  - Benefits for heart and mind: Salah is a comprehensive form of Allah's Dhikr. It will provide peace to the heart and mind. Pondering on the Qur'an read in Salah will increase our Imaan, intellect, and wisdom. Thinking about Aakhirah will free our heart and mind from the worldly worries.
  - Physical benefits: Cleanliness through Wudoo, exercise for the body such as going for and coming from Salah, bowing, bending, prostrating, sitting, etc.
  - Time management: Sleeping early to get up early for Fajr and developing a habit of punctuality for attending every Salah. Planning daily tasks according to the Salah schedule.
  - Social benefits: Salah helps us bind together as friends, neighbours, and relatives. For example, every day we will be meeting with our neighbors, getting information about them and if required, a chance to help and assist them. This will help us to develop a better and a united society.
  - Most important benefit: We will achieve eternal success in the Hereafter, InshaAllah.

One of the reasons for this reminder of success is that a person avoids coming to Salah because he thinks that he will lose worldly gains associated with work if he comes to Salah. He sometimes behaves like a foolish person who is running in a direction opposite to the real one.

Allah is the Greatest. Allah is the Greatest.	(There is) no god except Allah
اَللهُ أَكْبَرُ اَللهُ أَكْبَرُ	لَا إِلٰهَ إِلَّا اللهُ.

- Adhaan ends with its starting words. The starting message was: Come towards Salah keeping in mind Allah's Greatness.
- The message at the end is: If you don't come to Salah, you will be the loser. Allah will still be the Greatest and the one truly worthy of worship. If you come, then you will please the one who is the Greatest and the true God, thereby achieving the real success.

Lesson 6a — Fajr Adhaan, Iqamah, & Du'aa After Wudoo

After completing this lesson (a & b), you will learn **63 new** words, which occur **23,267** times in the Qur'an.

In the Adhaan of the Fajr, we say the following words two times after حَيَّ عَلَى الْفَلَاحِ:

مِّنَ النَّوْمِ.	خَيۡرٌ	³ اَلصَّلٰوةُ
than sleep.	is better	Salah

(ابوداؤد:501)

> Sleep is similar to death and Salah is the real life!
> Sleep is call of our self and Salah is the call of Allah.
> Sleep is comfort for our body and Salah is the comfort for our soul. Sleeping at the time of Fajr is harmful for our health too. Most of the heart or brain attacks happen in the morning hours. Freshness of the morning is the best remedy for a healthy body.
> Salah gives us a sense of happiness, calms our agitated nerves, and relaxes the mind, body, and soul.

Iqamah: When the Jama'ah (group) starts praying, the words of Adhaan are repeated. After حَيَّ عَلَى الْفَلَاحِ the words قَدْ قَامَتِ الصَّلٰوةُ (certainly the Salah is established) are repeated twice. Iqamah is a call to join Salah for those who are already in Masjid and waiting for the Salah to start.

قَامَتِ اَلصَّلٰوةُ	⁴⁰⁶ قَدۡ
the Salah is established.	Certainly

Du'aa for starting Wudoo is: بِسْمِ الله.

Du'aa after completing the Wudoo is given below: The Messenger of Allah ﷺ said, "Whoever of you performs Wudoo' carefully and then affirms this the eight gates of Jannah are opened for him. He may enter through whichever of these gates he desires (to enter)." (Tirmidhi)

اللهُ	إِلَّا	إِلٰهَ	لَا	أَنۡ	أَشۡهَدُ
Allah.	except	God	(there is) no	that	I bear witness
			لَا: no, مَا: no, what		شَهَادَة، شَهِيۡد

> Explanation of this was given earlier in the lesson on Adhaan.
> Remember death. The Prophet ﷺ said: "He whose last words are: لَا إِلٰهَ إِلَّا الله will enter Jannah. (Abu Dawood) "Exhort your dying men to recite: لَا إِلٰهَ إِلَّا الله". (Muslim)
> An emergency doctor who was serving in an Arab country said that during his service he has seen several people dying but only one or two were able to recite لَا إِلٰهَ إِلَّا الله at their last breath. May Allah help us recite لَا إِلٰهَ إِلَّا الله and do His Dhikr more often so that we get a chance to say لَا إِلٰهَ إِلَّا الله at our death.

لَهُ	لَا شَرِيكَ	وَحْدَهُ
to Him.	(there is) no partner	He is alone,
	شَرِيكَ، شُرَكَاء، شِرْك، مُشْرِك	وَاحِد، أَحَد، تَوْحِيد

- Allah's oneness is again repeated here along with the rejection of any partnership with Allah. This emphasis is important because Allah will never forgive those who do شِرْك (Shirk), i.e., associating partners with Allah.
- Recite this keeping in mind the dangerous consequences of Shirk.

وَرَسُولُهُ	عَبْدُهُ	مُحَمَّدًا	أَنَّ	وَأَشْهَدُ
and His Messenger.	(is) His slave	Muhammad ﷺ	that	I bear witness
ه / رَسُولُ / وَ	ه / عَبْدُ	The meaning of the word محمد is: one who is praised a lot.	أَنْ، أَنَّ	شَهَادَة : Witness
messenger / and	slave		that	

- Explanation of this part was given in the Adhaan lesson. The word "slave" is added here. Previous nations such as Christians had raised their Prophet (Isa ﷺ) to the level of God by making him Allah's son. Allah and His messenger, Prophet Muhammad ﷺ want us to be safe from such Shirk. Therefore we are asked to repeat these words in our Salah.
- Allah made us and we are for Him. He owns us and everything else. We are all slaves of Allah and should live like a true slave. The best slave of Allah is Prophet Muhammad ﷺ. He is a model for us, how a true slave should be.

الْمُتَطَهِّرِينَ.	مِنَ	وَاجْعَلْنِي	التَّوَّابِينَ	مِنَ	اجْعَلْنِي	اَللّٰهُمَّ
those who purify themselves	from among	and make me	those who repent	from among	Make me	O Allah!
مُتَطَهِّر ← مُتَطَهِّرُونَ، مُتَطَهِّرِينَ		نِي / اجْعَلْ / وَ	تَوَّاب ← تَوَّابُونَ، تَوَّابِينَ		نِي / اجْعَلْ	
		me / make / and			me / Make	

- We humans commit mistakes again and again. We do many things that we are not supposed to do. We don't do things that we are supposed to do and if we do, we don't do them properly. Therefore we need to repent again and again.
- Conditions for Tawbah (repentance) are: Give up the sin, regret having done it, resolve never to go back to it, and return all the things unlawfully grabbed from others.
- Pruity means purity in our beliefs, thoughts, body, clothes, and places. O Allah! Make us pure in every aspect.

After completing this lesson (a & b), you will learn **80 new** words, which occur 26,082 times in the Qur'an.

Things to pronounce when bowing (رُكُوع):

107		41
الْعَظِيمِ ❁	رَبِّيَ	سُبْحَانَ
the Magnificent	my Lord,	Glory be to

Try to imagine and feel the four things mentioned here:

➤ My Rabb is free from any defects or imperfections. He does not need any partner or help. He is not an oppressor or unjust. He has not created anything in vain. He neither gets tired nor slumbers. He is not weak and doesn't fear anyone. There is no flaw in His commands. I do not have any complain for the tests in my life.

➤ He is Rabb, i.e., who takes care of all of me and everything around me. He is the Cherisher, Sustainer, and Provider of everything that I need. He is the one who controls each and every one of my 1 trillion cells every second of my life. He is continuously supplying and feeding me with oxygen. He is smoothly running all my body systems such as the blood system and digestion system.

➤ You are addressing Allah saying: My Rabb. If your mother says: "my son is very good" or "my daughter is very good" right in front of you, what does it show? It shows her love and affection! Say it with love when you do Tasbeeh in Rukoo'.

➤ He is magnificent عَظِيم. No one can overpower or put pressure on him.

حَمِدَهُ ❁		لِمَنْ		سَمِعَ اللهُ
praised Him		to the one who		Allah has listened
هُ	حَمِدَ	مَنْ	لِ	
Him	praised	the one who	for, to	

➤ Allah listens to everyone. Here it means that Allah responds to the one who praises Him and answers his prayers.

➤ Allah does not need our praise for Him. It does not benefit him at all. He does not lose anything if we don't praise Him. Only we benefit by praising Him.

الْحَمْدُ ❁	وَلَكَ	رَبَّنَا
is all praise.	and for You only	O our Lord!

➤ We can praise and thank Allah from the depth of our heart if we just keep in mind the meaning of رَبَّنَا while saying it.

➤ Hamd حَمْد has two meanings: praising and giving thanks. Glorify Allah whole heartedly, with the feelings of gratitude and praise.

➤ Say it with 3 feelings: You are Rabb; Our Rabb; Hamd belong to You only.

➤ Visualize His best qualities: O Allah! You are the most Merciful, the Most Powerful, the Best Creator, and the Best Designer. Say it from the depth of your heart.

One more Dhikr of Rukoo':

The Messenger of Allah ﷺ used to say this while raising his head from Rukoo':

"سَمِعَ اللهُ لِمَنْ حَمِدَهُ، رَبَّنَا وَلَكَ الْحَمْدُ مِلْءَ السَّمَوَاتِ وَمِلْءَ الْأَرْضِ وَمِلْءَ مَا بَيْنَهُمَا وَمِلْءَ مَا شِئْتَ مِنْ شَيْءٍ بَعْدُ" (Tirmidhi).

Meanings of the remaining part are given below.

filling the skies	and filling the earth	and filling what is	in between them,
مِلْءَ السَّمٰوٰتِ	وَمِلْءَ الْأَرْضِ	وَمِلْءَ مَا	بَيْنَهُمَا،
1	310	461	266

and filling	all those things what	You will	from anything	after (them).
وَمِلْءَ	مَا	شِئْتَ	مِنْ شَيْءٍ	بَعْدُ،
	3		283	198

> The words of this Dhikr are amazing. Look at the life of the Messenger of Allah ﷺ. He passed through continuous trials and tribulations. He did not have even two full consecutive meals in his life. In addition to that, he was persecuted for almost 13 years in Makkah and was attacked by armies for several years in Madinah. Keep this in mind and look at the words of this Dhikr expressing thanks and gratitude to Allah! No human can reach even a fraction of what the Prophet ﷺ had expressed in these words. His actions indeed were far superior to his words.

> According to modern research, one has to be full of gratitude for a peaceful and satisfactory life. One of the modern success expert had suggested that in order to develop gratitude, we should try to imagine filling our body with the liquid of gratitude every night before sleep! As if every part of our body is swimming in gratitude.

> Now look at the words of the Prophet ﷺ. He wants to fill up the heavens and the earth and everything in between with gratitude and praise to Allah!

> The last part of the Dhikr are more amazing! After mentioning heavens and the earth, he says that he would like to thank and praise Allah by filling "whatever You will O Allah!". That means, O Allah, I know heavens and earth only. If there is anything beyond that which pleases You, I would love to fill that too with gratitude and praise! Allah know best.

> Indeed the modern success experts and trainers can't reach even the dust of what the Prophet ﷺ has taught us about gratitude.

Adhkaar of Sajdah (سَجْدَة):

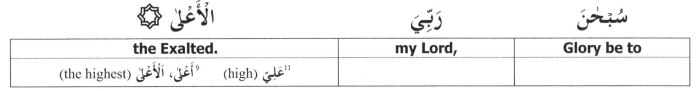

Glory be to	my Lord,	the Exalted. 🔹 الْأَعْلَى
سُبْحٰنَ	رَبِّيَ	
		(high) عَلِيّ¹¹ (the highest) أَعْلَى، الْأَعْلَى⁹

Position of Sajdah: Sajdah (prostration) is the expression of complete submission to Allah. Try to imagine and feel the four things mentioned here. (1) Allah is free from defects; (2) He is Rabb; (3) He is my Rabb; and (4) He is الْأَعْلَى, i.e., the highest, the topmost. I am in the lowest position on this earth and my Rabb is the highest on His Throne. We are nearest to Allah in the position of Sajdah.

The message of Tasbeeh: Latest research shows that we need to have two things for a successful and happy life: Positive attitude and gratitude. We have learned about gratitude. The standing in every Rakah of our Salah starts with اَلْحَمْدُ لِلهِ and ends with وَلَكَ الْحَمْدُ. Now let us see Tasbeeh:

➢ We recite Tasbeeh at least 9 times in every Rakah, and therefore more than 200 times every day. The most recited Dhikr in Salah is سُبْحٰنَ رَبِّيْ. Remember, Allah wants us to repeat this for a special reason: to train us how to think and live every day in the best way.

➢ سُبْحٰنَ رَبِّيْ has many dimensions for our training. Most important among them is that Allah does not need any partners. It also means that the commandments of Allah like Salah, Fasting, Hijab etc. are faultless because Allah Himself is free from all defects.

➢ Allah has kept many things to test us like the design of our nose, face, physique, family, country, and its situation, etc. These tests are also faultless. As an obedient slave, we must say: O Allah! Help us fulfill our duties without any complaint against You. Solve our problems and correct our conditions in order to achieve success in this world and in the Hereafter.

➢ While reciting Tasbeeh, we bow down and we put our face on earth and say رَبِّي with love and affection. As if we are saying, O Allah! We submit to you completely and do not have any complaint. If we do Tasbeeh with this feeling and manner then we can develop a strong positive attitude. The present day "Success Experts" cannot give even 1% of it.

➢ Remember, whatever Allah does is perfect. The situation we are in is either a test and/or due to our own faults. We should pray to Allah to help us do our best in whatever situation we are in or change it the best way. This is the secret of success.

To bring it into our lives, we need to apply the following formula:

• Ask: O Allah! Help me to accept every test of my life and not have any complaint against You. Never should I say: Why did this happen to me?

• Evaluate: How many times do I complain about my color, nose, face, physique, family, weather, country, environment, etc.?

• Plan: I will try to never have any negative feelings about my tests!

• Propagate. I will convey this to others.

Lesson 8a · Tashahhud

After completing this lesson (a & b), you will learn **93 new** words, which occur 27,536 times in the Qur'an.

46				6
وَالطَّيِّبَاتُ	وَالصَّلَوَاتُ	لِلّٰهِ		اَلتَّحِيَّاتُ
and the pure (deeds)	and the prayers	are due to Allah		All the compliments
		اللّٰه	لِ	
		Allah	for	
طَيِّبَةٌ، طَيِّبَات⁺	صَلَاةٌ، صَلَوَات⁺			تَحِيَّةٌ، تَحِيَّات⁺

➤ **All the compliments or all types of worship by a tongue:** Salah, Dhikr, Tilawah, Dawah, nice words, preaching, guiding, suggestions, etc.

➤ **All the prayers:** These include all types of worship such as Salah, Saum (fasting), training, helping, educating, and to go for Dawah and propagation.

➤ **All pure (deeds):** Pure words and actions that are not corrupted by wrong niyyah; actions that are not corrupted by Haram/wrong elements. They also include pure spending for Hajj, Zakah, Sadaqah (charity), etc.

Once the Prophet ﷺ said that seventy thousand people will enter Jannah without being taken to account or torment. He then described their attributes. Among other things, he said that they will keep trust in their Rabb (Allah). On hearing this 'Ukashah bin Mihsan (RA) stood up and requested: "Pray to Allah to make me one of them." The Prophet ﷺ said, "You are one of them." Then another man stood up and asked the same thing. The Prophet ﷺ answered, "'Ukashah has surpassed you."

[Al-Bukhari and Muslim]

➤ The Hadith teaches us that the moment we hear of any good, ask Allah for it, or else someone else will take the lead. Further, in the light of this Du'aa, we must check our past and draw a plan for the future.

➤ Three acts of worship are mentioned here. We can ask: O Allah! Help us participate in all these types of worship. And then evaluate: How are we using our tongue, our brain, our intellect, and most importantly, where are we spending our wealth? Make a plan to do these things properly and then propagate the idea.

3			114			75	42	
وَبَرَكَاتُهُ			وَرَحْمَتُ اللّٰه			أَيُّهَا النَّبِيُّ	عَلَيْكَ	اَلسَّلَامُ
and His blessings			and the Mercy of Allah			O Prophet!	be on you	Peace
هٗ	بَرَكَاتُ	وَ	اللّٰه	رَحْمَتُ	وَ	نَبِيُّونَ⁺، نَبِيِّينَ⁺،		
His	blessings	and	Allah	Mercy	and	أَنْبِيَآء⁺		
بَرَكَةٌ، بَرَكَات⁺			رَحِيمٌ: Continually Merciful			Prophets		

➤ Who performed the three types of worship (by using tongue, body, and spending) the best way? Of course, Prophet Muhammad ﷺ. He has also taught us what they are and how to do them. Therefore, we are praying for three things to be granted to him:

➤ سَلَام : Protection from any harm.

➤ رَحْمَة: Allah's blessings. May Allah take care of you with love and kindness.

➤ بَرَكَة : Continuity and increase in all blessings, favors, bounties, and goodness.

These three things are in a nice order. From example, if you plant a flower seed, you want to protect (سَلَام) it from insects, then give water (رَحْمَة), and then give manure (بَرَكَة) to help it grow bigger and stronger.

➤ Without protection, blessings (رَحْمَة) and increase (بَرَكَة) will be lost!

➤ **Explanation of Assalamu Alaikum (with each other):** اَلسَّلَام means all peace, just like اَلْحَمْدُ means all praise. It means, may Allah protect you from any harm. May Allah protect your Deen, Imaan, health, wealth, business, job, etc. May Allah save you from deficiencies, defects and undesired situations or things.

➤ If you add وَرَحْمَةُ اللهِ وَبَرَكَاتُه in your Salam, then it means: May Allah take care of you with love and kindness and grant you and increase you in His blessings!

➤ What a great way it is in comparison to mere hello, hi, or good morning. Furthermore, we get rewards by saying Assalamu Alaikum and the reward for practising a Sunnah.

125

اَلسَّلَامُ	عَلَيْنَا	وَعَلٰى	عِبَادِ اللهِ	الصَّالِحِينَ،
Peace	be on us	and on	the slaves of Allah,	the righteous ones.
	عَلَى : on	وَ : and	عَبْدُ اللهِ : Slave of Allah	صَالِح ← صَالِحُونَ، صَالِحِينَ
	نَا : Us	عَلٰى : On	عِبَادُ اللهِ : Slaves of Allah	

➤ Who received the favors of Allah? (1) Prophets; (2) Truthful people (Siddiqeen); (3) Martyrs (Shuhada); and (4) the Righteous (Saliheen).

➤ The prayer for peace is for the Prophet ﷺ, then for us, and then for the righteous ones. For Prophets and for the righteous people, inshaAllah, the Du'aa will be answered. We are in the middle of the two groups, and we hope that Allah will grant peace and protection for us too.

➤ Remember, Allah bestows His mercy on those who earn it, by acting upon the good and begging for mercy, like the righteous people did.

➤ Millions of people recite this Du'aa every day. If we want to receive their Du'aa then we should try to become Saliheen (pious). O Allah! Make us among the Saliheen so we can get the benefits of their Du'aa.

➤ Make a plan to become pious and to be in the company of Saliheen.

أَشْهَدُ	أَنْ	لَا إِلٰهَ	إِلَّا	اللهُ
I bear witness	that	(there is) no god	except	Allah.

➤ As mentioned earlier, a doctor who was serving in the emergency ward in an Arab country said that during his service he saw several people dying but only a few were able to say لَا إِلٰهَ إِلَّا اللهُ at their last breath. A son asked his father who was close to death to recite لَا إِلٰهَ إِلَّا اللهُ but the father couldn't. The son asked his father in Arabic "Please repeat لَا إِلٰهَ إِلَّا اللهُ after me". His father who was an Arab replied in Arabic, "Son! I want to say it but I am not able to". May Allah forgive him and forgive us and give us Tawfeeq to say it before we die.

➤ We don't know which Salah could be our last one. Inside the Salah, this could be the last declaration of لَا إِلٰهَ إِلَّا اللهُ. So recite it from the depth of heart and with full attention so that we get a chance to recite it before our death. The Prophet ﷺ said that he whose last words are لَا إِلٰهَ إِلَّا اللهُ would enter Jannah.

➤ How many times have we obeyed the desires of our Nafs (self)? If we did that, we made our Nafs our إِلٰه (god)! How many times have we obeyed Shaitaan? Obeying him is like worshipping him. Why did we do this? Due to bad friends or evil use of gadgets like (mobile, laptop, internet etc.) or due to laziness and lethargy? Let us ask Allah that He gives us Tawfeeq to use our time and resources in the right manner.

وَرَسُوْلُهُ.	عَبْدُهُ	مُحَمَّدًا	أَنَّ	وَأَشْهَدُ
and His Messenger.	is His slave	Muhammad	That	and I bear witness

- The explanation for the above is already given in Lesson No. 7 for Adhaan. The words عَبْدُهُ وَرَسُوْلُهُ are also explained in Lesson No. 8. The following paragraph is repeated for emphasis.
- Allah made us and we are for Him. He owns us and everything else. We are all slaves of Allah and should live like a true slave. The best slave of Allah is Prophet Muhammad ﷺ. He is a model for us, how a true slave should be. He is a model because he is a Messenger too.
- Allah says: وَكَذٰلِكَ جَعَلْنٰكُمْ أُمَّةً وَّسَطًا لِّتَكُوْنُوْا شُهَدَآءَ عَلَى النَّاسِ (and thus We have made you a middle nation that you may be witnesses to the people). (Al-Baqarah: 143)
- We are given a huge responsibility after the Messenger of Allah ﷺ to be a witness to the people, i.e., to convey to them what Islam is. This task is reminded in Tashahud of every Salah and in all five Adhaans and Iqamahs.

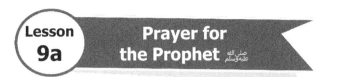

Lesson **9a** — **Prayer for the Prophet** ﷺ

After completing this lesson (a & b), you will learn **102 new** words, which occur **27,926** times in the Qur'an.

To pray for the Prophet ﷺ effectively, remember the sacrifices of our Prophet ﷺ for spreading the message of Islam. If we are Muslims **1500** years after his time and that too in a place far away from Makkah, then it is due to the blessing of Allah and after that due to his sacrifices.

Let us take an incident from his life. In spite of being extremely tired after doing Da'wah all day, he went to a tribe late in the evening. I should think that perhaps Islam reached me through that tribe. Along similar lines, I can feel the effect of every sacrifice on me and my life.

What can I do now in return for his sacrifices? Invite him for a dinner? Send him a gift? Nothing! I can only pray for him.

The Prophet ﷺ will receive the rewards from Allah anyway, whether I pray for him or not. It is in fact a great honor for me to pray for him. Furthermore, we receive rewards on praying for him! Everyone who prays for the Prophet ﷺ will receive in return ten rewards from Allah [Muslim].

26		2	5
الِ مُحَمَّدٍ	وَّعَلٰى عَلٰى مُحَمَّدٍ	صَلِّ	اَللّٰهُمَّ
the family of Muhammad,	**and on** | **on Muhammad**	**Send peace**	**O Allah!**
الِ: family, followers	عَلٰى | وَّ | مُحَمَّدٍ | عَلٰى	صَلِّ عَلٰى: Send peace	
أَهل: family	on | and | | on	صَلِّ: Pray	

➤ صَلِّ عَلٰى actually means: O Allah! Shower Your mercy on him, be very kind to him, raise his name, and elevate his position.

➤ O Allah! The Prophet ﷺ has done too many favors for us. We don't have anything to pay him back. Only You can reward him the best.

➤ الِ has two meanings: family and followers. If we take the second meaning, then this prayer is for us, the followers, too.

69				
الِ إِبْرَاهِيْمَ	وَعَلٰى	عَلٰى إِبْرَاهِيْمَ	صَلَّيْتَ	كَمَا
the family of Ibrahim.	**and on**	**on Ibrahim**	**You sent peace**	**as**
	عَلٰى | وَ		فَعَلْتَ: you did	كَ، كَمَا: as
	on | and		صَلَّيْتَ: you sent peace	

➤ O Allah! You gave Ibrahim عليه السلام such a position and leadership that all Muslims, Christians, and Jews accept him as a Prophet. O Allah! Give Prophet Muhammad ﷺ also such a status that all the people on this planet accept him as Your last prophet.

4	17	
مَّجِيْدٌ.	حَمِيْدٌ	إِنَّكَ
full of glory.	**worthy of praise,**	**Indeed, You are**
مَجْد: glory, splendor, magnificence	حَمْد: praise	كَ | إِنَّ
مَجِيْد: full of glory	حَمِيْد: worthy of praise	You | indeed, certainly

- O Allah! You have done a huge favor for us. You sent an excellent prophet for us. You are so Kind and so Merciful. You took so much care for our welfare. You are indeed worthy of praise and full of glory.
- O Allah! You are full of glory and splendor. You have all the resources. Therefore, You alone can give the best reward to the Prophet ﷺ.

Let us study the second part in which only two words are new: بَارِكْ and بَارَكْتَ.

اَللّٰهُمَّ	بَارِكْ	عَلٰى مُحَمَّدٍ	وَّعَلٰى	الِ مُحَمَّدٍ
O Allah!	Send blessings	on Muhammad	and on	the family of Muhammad;

- In the first part صَلِّ عَلٰى is mentioned which includes بَرَكَة also. However, in supplications, we repeat the request in different words to express our attachment with the Prophet ﷺ.
- The meaning of *Barakah* is benediction and blessings. It also includes the continuity of andincrease in these blessings forever.
- *Barakah* in actions imply their acceptance and getting excellent rewards for them.
- *Barakah* in family implies its growth, prosperity, expansion, and continuity over generations.
- The prayer for *Barakah* is for the family of Prophet Muhammad ﷺ and for his followers too. May Allah make us true followers of Prophet Muhammad ﷺ.

كَمَا	بَارَكْتَ	عَلٰى إِبْرَاهِيمَ	وَعَلٰى	الِ إِبْرَاهِيمَ
as	You sent blessings	on Ibrahim	and on	the family of Ibrahim.

إِنَّكَ	حَمِيْدٌ	مَّجِيْدٌ.
Indeed, You are	worthy of praise,	full of glory.

O Allah! You gave Ibrahim عليه السلام such a position and leadership that all the Muslims, Christians, and Jews accept him as a prophet. O Allah! Give Prophet Muhammad ﷺ also such a status that all the people on this planet accept him as Your last prophet.

While praying for the Prophet ﷺ, remember his sacrifices for us. Remember also that he was sent as a teacher of the Qur'an.

Ask: O Allah! Help me become his student, i.e., study the Qur'an and Hadith regularly.

Evaluate: How much time do I spend learning these two things? Do I say that "I am busy and I have no time for it?" No time to become the student of Prophet, ﷺ? Do we really love him?

Plan: Fix a time for learning the Qur'an and Hadith daily.

Propagate: Try your best to spread the teachings of the Qur'an and Sunnah.

Try to recall the advice of the Prophet ﷺ while praying for him. For example, regarding the Qur'an, he said: Convey from me, even if it is one verse (that you know).

- How can we convey if we don't understand it? Therefore, make a serious plan to understand the complete Qur'an so that we can answer non-Muslims' questions, address misconceptions and guide people towards Islam, InshaAllah.
- Imagine that you are lost in a desert. Your food and supplies are finished and you are getting close to death. Suddenly a man comes to you with food and drink. You enjoy the food, get your energy back and start thanking him. He asks you to help him in distributing the food to other 'dying people.' You just stand there and keep repeating, "May Allah have mercy on you, and may Allah bless you." Won't it be a very rude and thankless attitude? Extend this example to our relationship with the Prophet ﷺ. If we just pray for the Prophet ﷺ and don't convey the message to others, will the Prophet ﷺ be happy with us?
- Make efforts to increase your love towards Prophet ﷺ by reading about his life and by following his Sunnah.

Lesson **10a** **Prayers after Salah**

After completing this lesson (a & b), you will learn **116 new** words, which occur 28,854 times in the Qur'an.

Introduction: Different prayers are recited after Salah. Two of them are given here.

حَسَنَةً	فِى الدُّنْيَا	اِتِنَا		رَبَّنَآ
(that which is) good	**in (this) world**	**Give us**		**Our Lord!**
حَسَن: good (masculine)		نَا	اٰتِ	
حَسَنَة: good (feminine)		us	Give	

Many Du'aas (supplications) begin with word Rabbana (O our Rabb!).
Rabb is the one who takes care of us, fulfills all our needs every second, and helps us grow.

"Good" in this world includes the following:
➢ Necessities of life such as sound health, prosperous family, children, friends, respect, honor, wealth, job, business, etc.
➢ Peace, security, and tranquility in which we can follow the commandments of Allah.
➢ Things which will be of help to us in the Hereafter such as beneficial knowledge, correct faith (Aqeedah), good deeds, sincerity, good manners, good upbringing etc.
➢ Nothing is "good" from the first category (health, family, children, wealth, etc.) if it destroys our Hereafter.

Let us apply the formula to bring this Du'aa into our lives. We have already asked Allah for Hasanaat. Now let us do the next three steps.
➢ **Evaluate:** Are things that I am running after in this life be counted as حَسَنَة? If I ask for something of this life and I don't get it, am I satisfied with Allah's decision?
➢ **Plan:** Prepare a schedule of activities for everyday as a first thing in the morning so that we get the Hasanaat.
➢ **Propagate:** Convey the message of this verse to others.

حَسَنَةً	الْاٰخِرَةِ	وَّفِى
(that which is) good	**the Hereafter,**	**and in**
	اٰخِرَة: last (feminine), اٰخِر: last (masculine)	وَ + فِي

"Good" in the Hereafter includes the following:
➢ Allah's pleasure;
➢ Paradise;
➢ Closeness to our beloved Prophet, Muhammad ﷺ
➢ Closeness to other prophets, truthful people, martyrs, and pious people; and
➢ Being able to see Allah is the biggest 'Hasanah' of the Hereafter.

(of) the Fire.	the punishment	and protect us from		
نَار : Fire النَّار : the Fire (hellfire)		نَا	قِ	وَ
		us	protect	and

➤ Entry into Jannah does not always guarantee the freedom from hellfire. The scholars say that if a believer's sins outweigh his good deeds, he will be sent into the hellfire first so that he is cleansed of all his sins.

➤ The easiest way to erase the sins is to do Istighfaar (ask for His forgiveness) as much as possible. Pain, sufferings, and difficulties in a believer's life also remove his sins.

➤ May Allah forgive our sins and give us the ability and the passion to do good deeds and save us from the Fire.

A Very Important Du'aa (Prayer) After Salah

Mu'adh bin Jabal (May Allah be pleased with him) reported: Messenger of Allah ﷺ held my hand and said, "O Mu'adh, By Allah, I love you and advise you not to miss supplicating after every Salah (prayer) saying: اَللّٰهُمَّ أَعِنِّيْ عَلٰى ذِكْرِكَ وَشُكْرِكَ وَحُسْنِ عِبَادَتِك. [Abu Dawood and An-Nasa'i]

	13		1			
وَحُسْنِ عِبَادَتِكَ.		وَشُكْرِكَ		عَلٰى ذِكْرِكَ	أَعِنِّيْ	اَللّٰهُمَّ
and to worship You in the best possible way.		and to give thanks to You		to remember You	Help me	O Allah!
حُسْنِ عِبَادَتِكَ the best of your worship		وَ + شُكُرِكَ and your thanks		عَلٰى + ذِكْرِكَ on your remembrance	أَعِنْ + نِيْ	

Realize first the importance of the Du'aa. Look at the emphasis given by the Prophet ﷺ to this Du'aa. He first held the hand of Mua'dh (RA) and then said: I love you. Then he said: I advise you.

We can recite this Du'aa with different feelings. For example:

➤ O Allah! Although I just finished this Salah, I could not offer it in the very best way. Help me to perform it better next time.

➤ O Allah! Help me thank You for giving me the opportunity to worship You.

➤ O Allah! Help me remember You after the Salah, when I will be busy with worldly affairs outside the Masjid. Help me to thank You when I receive different benefits in my worldly affairs and dealings.

➤ Help me live my whole life in such a way that it becomes full of Your worship.

➤ حُسْنِ عِبَادَتِكَ: We offer Salah but very fast, without proper focus, and without feelings and sometimes with laziness. O Allah! Help us offer our worship in a way that pleases You.

| Lesson 11a | Surah Al-Ikhlaas |

After completing this lesson (a & b), you will learn **131 new** words, which occur **30,797** times in the Qur'an.

Introduction: This is a small but very important Surah. When you recite this Surah in the Salah, do not do so just because it is a small Surah but keep in mind its significance and importance also.

- The name of this Surah is Al-Ikhlaas (the purification). Whoever recites this Surah with understanding and believes in what is mentioned in it, his faith will become pure and free from any Shirk (polytheism) or any wrong concepts.
- It is equivalent to one-third of the Qur'an.
- It answers the most fundamental question: Who should we worship and who can qualify to be God.
- It was the Sunnah of the Prophet ﷺ to recite this Surah along with the last two Surahs of the Qur'an once after every obligatory (*Fard*) Salah and thrice after Fajr and Maghrib Salahs.

﷽ اَعُوْذُ بِاللهِ مِنَ الشَّيْطٰنِ الرَّجِيْمِ ﷽ بِسْمِ اللهِ الرَّحْمٰنِ الرَّحِيْمِ ﷽

① أَحَدٌ ⁷⁴	اللّٰهُ	هُوَ	قُلْ ³³²
the One and Unique	**(is) Allah,**	**He**	**Say:**
One وَاحِد One and only أَحَد	He is Allah: هُوَ الله		

(Say) قُلْ³³² (They said) قَالُوْا³³² (He said) قَالَ⁵³⁰

➤ Allah is alone. Let us take four important aspects of His Oneness with examples:
  ① He is alone in His entity. He has no partners or relatives, no son or father.
  ② He is alone in His attributes. Nobody has knowledge of the unseen, no one can hear, help, or see the way Allah does.
  ③ He is alone in His rights. For example, only He has the right to be worshipped.
  ④ He is alone in His powers. For example, He alone has the right to declare something lawful or unlawful, permissible or impermissible.

Let us apply the following simple formula to bring this Surah into our lives:
➤ **Du'aa/Ask:** O Allah! Help me worship You alone.
➤ **Evaluate:** How many times did I follow my desires? According to the Qur'an, following one's own desire is to make it god [45:23]. How many times did I succumb to the whisperings of the Shaitaan? According to the Qur'an, following Shaitaan is like worshipping him [23:60]. Why did I listen to him? Because of bad company, TV, internet, or just laziness?
➤ **Plan:** Remove bad things, bad friends, and bad habits and plan to use the things properly.
➤ **Propagate:** This verse starts with "Qul." We must propagate the message of Islam to others with wisdom and kindness, like the way Prophet Mohammed ﷺ did. Use this Surah to spread the message of Tawheed and Ikhlaas (sincerity).

② الصَّمَدُ ¹	اللّٰهُ
the Self-Sufficient.	**Allah,**
الصَّمَد: Everyone needs him, He needs no one.	This is Allah's original name. The rest are names like Ar-Raheem that show His attributes.

- Allah is As-Samad, i.e., He does not need any person or anything. He does not sleep nor gets tired nor does he need anything.
- Everyone needs Him. Realize that there are billions of creatures including human beings that are alive because of His mercy, kindness, and continuous support.
- We can also pray to Allah: O Allah! You alone have been fulfilling my needs in past, so please continue to fulfill them in the future also! O Allah! Make me dependent upon You alone and not upon anyone else.

is He begotten,	and nor	He did neither beget	
يَلِد : begets (active voice)	لَمْ : did not	يَلِدْ	لَمْ
يُولَدُ : is begotten (passive voice)	لَنْ 106: will not	beget	He did not

- This ayah means that Allah was there forever and will be there forever. Try to go back thousands, millions, and billions of years in time and think!! He was always there. Do the same thing for future, and He will always be there.
- Why do we have children? Because when we are tired or feel lonely, they cheer us up. When we grow old, they take care of us. When we die, they continue our plans and our ambitions. Allah is free from all such weaknesses and needs.
- While reciting this ayah we should feel the responsibility of conveying this message to over two billion Christians who wrongly believe that Jesus عليه السلام is the son of Allah.

anyone.	comparable	unto Him	and (there) is not		
		and none is comparable to Him.			
أَحَد : One (used for Allah only)	equal	for Him, unto Him	يَكُنْ	لَمْ	وَ
أَحَد : anyone (used negatively, like here)			is	not	and

- Nobody is equal or comparable to Allah in His Entity, His attributes, His Rights, and His Powers.
- Try to imagine the vastness of this universe, billions of kilometers wide; and no one exists there except Allah's creation.
- **Du'aa:** O Allah! Help me develop a strong faith that You are enough for me in all matters of life.
- **Evaluate:** Do I remember this aspect when I am in presence of powerful people? Do I expect benefits from someone else? Is there anybody whom I am afraid of?
- **Plan:** Think deeply over the attributes of Allah and in the ayahs of the Qur'an so that Allah's greatness fills our minds.

Amazing Benefit of this Surah:

One of the companions of the Prophet صلى الله عليه وسلم used to recite Surah Al-Ikhlaas followed by some other Surah in every Raka'ah of Salah. When the Prophet عليه وسلم asked him about this, he said, "I love it very much." The Prophet صلى الله عليه وسلم said, "Your love for this Surah has made you enter Jannah." (Bukhari: 774)

How can we develop **the love of this Surah**? Here are some tips.

- We should thank Allah from the depth of our heart that he conveyed to us the clean, pure, and true message. We now know who is our Creator and what does he want from us. If I had not received this message, I would have been lost in bad thoughts and deeds. Therefore, we should love to recite this Surah.

- If you are an ordinary person and you have a very close relative or friend who is a famous sportsman or a leader, won't you happily mention his name when you introduce yourself to new people? Let us extend this argument. Allah is our Creator and our Sustainer. He created us and this whole wonderful world for us! His love for us is much more than that of a mother's love for her children! Then why shouldn't we love to mention His name and praise him often?
- Allah is such that there is none in comparison to Him in His creativity, in His wisdom, in His lordship, in His power, in His love, etc., most importantly, no one is like Him in His forgiveness and in His grants. People don't like the one who keeps slipping and falling; Allah loves to forgive. People hate if we ask them; Allah loves when we ask Him. No one is kind and caring like Allah is. Allah has 99 names describing His attributes. No one was, is, and will be like Him in all of these attributes.

Such feelings will InshaAllah help us in developing a love of Allah and reciting this Surah with love.

Lesson 12a — **Surah Al-Falaq**

After completing this lesson (a & b), you will learn **144 new** words, which occur **31,638** times in the Qur'an.

Introduction: Surah al-Falaq and Surah an-Nas, the last two Surahs teach us the excellent prayers to protect ourselves.

- It is the Sunnah of the Prophet ﷺ to recite the last three Surahs once after every Salah and thrice after Fajr and Maghrib.
- It has been reported by Ayesha (RA) that before sleeping, the Prophet ﷺ used to blow into his hands, recite the last three Surahs and then pass his hands over his body. [Bukhari and Muslim].

Who among us wants to get protection? Everyone! We should then make it a habit to recite these Surahs regularly. We get two benefits by doing so: (i) Get the protection, and (ii) receive the reward for following the Sunnah.

اَعُوْذُبِاللهِ مِنَ الشَّيْطٰنِ الرَّجِيْمِ ۞ بِسْمِ اللهِ الرَّحْمٰنِ الرَّحِيْمِ ۞

الْفَلَقِ ①ّ	بِرَبِّ	اَعُوْذُ	قُلْ
of the daybreak,	in (the) Lord	I seek refuge	Say:
فَلَق : daybreak	بِ + رَبّ	اَعُوْذُ بِاللهِ	

- ➤ We should constantly remember that we are surrounded by evil attacks day and night including those from viruses, mischief makers, and jealous people. While reciting this Surah, we should first realize that we are not safe and then beg Allah for protection.
- ➤ He is the Rabb of the daybreak. Think and study about the Sun, the source of daylight, its diameter of 1.4 million kilometers, its distance of 150 million kilometers and see how Allah rotates the earth with its circumference of 40000 kilometers around the sun to bring out the day and then realize the greatness of Allah while reciting this ayah.
- ➤ Allah brings out the day from the darkness of night. Similarly, Allah can remove from us the darkness of evil.
- ➤ The Surah starts with "Say." We should recite this Surah as well as convey it to others with wisdom and kindness, the same way that the Prophet ﷺ did.

خَلَقَ ②	مَا	شَرِّ	مِنْ
He created,	(of) that which	(the) evil	from
خَالِق : Creator	what; that which; not مَا دِيْنُكَ : What is your Deen?		

- ➤ شَرّ has two meanings: evil and suffering. Some evil things appear to be good but their end is suffering. Therefore they are also evil.
- ➤ We ask Allah's protection from the evil of what He has created, i.e., from the evil of His creations. For example, Allah created human beings to worship Him but some of them hurt others. We ask Allah to protect us from the evil of such persons.
- ➤ Likewise we ask Allah's protection from the evil of all living and non-living creatures.
- ➤ Allah is the Creator and the rest are His creations. We seek His help from the evil of His creations which include everything. However, the next three verses talk of three specific evils. One thing that is common to these three (night, magic, jealousy) is that we don't realize if these evils are working against us!

			1	423			1	
وَقَبَ ۝3		إِذَا		غَاسِقٍ		وَمِنْ شَرِّ		
it becomes intense,		**when**		**(of) darkness**		**and from the evil**		
وَقَبَ: it became intense		إِذْ:when				شَرِّ	مِنْ	وَ
إِذَا وَقَبَ:when it becomes intense		إِذَا: when				Evil	from	and

➤ After every **12** hours comes the night. The time for work is over and people are relatively free. It is the time when the human mind can easily be corrupted by the devil. An empty man's brain is a devil's workshop.

➤ Most of the evil, indecent, and immoral acts happen at night such as bad TV programs, evil parties, evil movies, and other evils.

➤ It is easier for the thieves and enemies to attack at night.

➤ Staying awake late is also evil because it becomes difficult to get up for Fajr. It is extremely harmful to health too. You lose the excellent opportunities of morning work.

	4		1			
فِى الْعُقَدِ ۝4		النَّفَّٰثَٰتِ		وَمِنْ شَرِّ		
in the knots,		**(of) those who blow**		**and from (the) evil**		
عُقْدَةٌ، عُقَد+: knot		نَفَّاثَةٌ: the one who blows (fg)				
		نَفَثْت+				

➤ Magic or sorcery is a big test from Allah. If the one who is affected by the magic doesn't have strong faith in Allah, he may start committing shirk and do unIslamic practices to find the solution.

➤ In some families where relations are not good, people are scared of visiting relatives. They are afraid of magic or other evils from them. This Surah is the best cure for all problems.

➤ Don't forget the daily blowing by the enemy who lives with us! The Prophet ﷺ said, "When any one of you sleeps, Satan ties three knots at the back of his neck. He recites this incantation at every knot: `You have a long night, so sleep.' If he awakes and remembers Allah, one knot is loosened. If he performs Wudoo, the (second) knot is loosened; and if he performs prayer, (all) knots are loosened and he begins his morning in a happy and refreshed mood; otherwise, he gets up in bad spirits and sluggish state." [Al-Bukhari, Muslim]

➤ If you stay awake late, you give a big chance to Shaitaan to make you sleep and miss Fajr.

	1		1			
حَسَدَ ۝5		إِذَا		حَاسِدٍ		وَمِنْ شَرِّ
he envies.		**when**		**(of) an envier**		**and from the evil**
حَسَدَ: he envied				فَاعِل: doer		
إِذَا حَسَدَ: when he envies				حَاسِد: the one who envies		

➤ If you receive something good, a jealous person wishes that you lose it and he gets it. If not, at least you should lose it. He will try to destroy your reputation, work, property or hurt you.

➤ Pray to Allah that we are never jealous of anyone. It is like objecting to Allah's distribution! Say A'oodhubillah and pray for more for him and for yourself. You will get it too! The Prophet ﷺ said, "Beware of envy because envy consumes (destroys) the virtues just as the fire consumes the firewood," or he said "grass." [Abu Dawud]

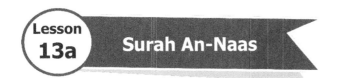

Lesson 13a — **Surah An-Naas**

After completing this lesson (a & b), you will learn **156 new** words, which occur **32,111** times in the Qur'an.

Study & Ponder — Propagate — Ask — Visualize Feel — Plan (Check with Scholars) — Evaluate

This is the last Surah of the Qur'an. The introduction to this Surah is given in the last lesson.

اَعُوْذُ بِاللهِ مِنَ الشَّيْطٰنِ الرَّجِيْمِ ۞ ۞ بِسْمِ اللهِ الرَّحْمٰنِ الرَّحِيْمِ ۞

النَّاسِ ①	بِرَبِّ	اَعُوْذُ	قُلْ
mankind	in the Lord (of)	I seek refuge	Say:
إِنْسَان : man	بِ + رَبّ	اَعُوْذُ بِاللهِ مِنَ الشَّيْطٰنِ الرَّجِيْمِ	
نَاس : mankind			

➤ **Visualize:** Allah is the Rabb of seven billion people living now on the planet, in addition to those who died before and those who will be coming in future.

➤ He is the one who causes the rain to fall, brings forth the crops, maintains the sun and the earth in their respective orbits, alters the seasons, and all other things for our survival.

➤ He looks after every cell and every atom of each one of us every second. He is all-time Rabb of everyone. **Feel** His greatness while reciting it.

➤ Allah starts the Surah with "Say." We should recite this Surah as well as convey it to others with wisdom and kindness, the same way that the Prophet ﷺ did.

145	13
اِلٰهِ النَّاسِ ③	مَلِكِ النَّاسِ ②
the God of mankind,	the King of mankind,

➤ مَلِك and مَلَك should not be mixed! The word مَلَك means angel (plural: مَلَائِكَة). The words مَلَك and مَلَائِكَة occur in the Qur'an **88** times.

➤ **Visualize:** He is the true King of seven billion people alive today. He owns everything they have, including their life and death. However much they deny or forget Him, they call upon Him, especially during tough times and difficulties.

➤ **Ask:** O Allah! Help me accept You as the true King and the only God in my daily life.

➤ **Evaluate:** How many times did I follow my desires? According to the Qur'an, following one's own desire is to make it god [45:23]. How many times did I succumb to the whisperings of the Shaitaan? According to the Qur'an, following Shaitaan is like worshipping him [36:60]. Why did I listen to him? Because of bad company, TV, internet?

➤ **Plan:** Remove bad friends, habits, and things from your life.

	1	
الْخَنَّاسِ ④	الْوَسْوَاسِ	مِنْ شَرِّ
the one who withdraws (after whispering),	(of) the whisperer	from (the) evil
	one who puts something secretly in the heart	

➤ Whisper is the first attack of Shaitaan. If he succeeds then the man intends to do bad thing. Shaitaan then pushes the man to do the bad thing. If this is repeated, it becomes a habit. Bad habits lead to bad end.

➤ Whenever we are careless, Shaitaan whispers. If we remember Allah, he withdraws. But he never gives up the whispering activity.

الَّذِىْ	يُوَسْوِسُ	فِىْ صُدُوْرِ	النَّاسِ ⑤
who	whispers	into the chests	(of) mankind,

the one who		whispers	يُوَسْوِسُ	صَدْر، صُدُوْر +	
الَّذِيْ عَلَّمَ بِالْقَلَمِ		one who whispers	وَسْوَاس		

> Shaitaan tries to whisper into the chest as the chest is the entry region of the 'heart.' This is similar to a thief entering through the open space around a house.
> If the heart is 'alive' and 'sound' with the Dhikr of Allah, then the whisper attacks of Shaitaan fail and he withdraws miserably. If not, the person falls into the sin.
> Allah says about the Qur'an: وَشِفَآءٌ لِّمَا فِى الصُّدُوْرِ , i.e., a healing for that which is in the chests [10:57]. There are many diseases of the heart such as ignorance, doubts, hypocrisy, evil desires, enmity, hatred, jealousy, etc.

مِنَ الْجِنَّةِ	وَالنَّاسِ ⑥
from among Jinns	and mankind.

> The Prophet ﷺ told that every one of us has a Shaitaan Jinn always with him/her. He continuously tries to mislead us at every possible opportunity by whispering.
> Who are the Shaitaans from humans? All those people who work for Shaitaan directly or indirectly, who seduce us away from Allah. They include most of our media, television, newspapers and magazines that create doubts about Islam or call towards materialism and immorality. In addition, there are men and women around us who through their dresses, talks, and actions work as agents of Shaitaan. Isn't the world full of such people? Do you now see how important this Surah is for our safety!
> In fact, a hadith mentions the greatness of the last two Surahs. 'Uqbah bin 'Amir said that the Messenger of Allah ﷺ said: 'O 'Uqbah, shall I not teach you the best two Surahs that can be recited?' And he taught me: قُلْ أَعُوْذُ بِرَبِّ الْفَلَقِ، قُلْ أَعُوْذُ بِرَبِّ النَّاسِ
> Plan: Try to avoid all bad programs, gadgets, and friends and use your time to do good things. In addition to seeking Allah's help, strive as a team to create a clean society free from evil things.

Lesson 14a — **Surah Al-Asr**

After completing this lesson (a & b), you will learn **174 new** words, which occur **36,556** times in the Qur'an.

Introduction: This small Surah provides mankind with a formula to avoid loss. The solution is to do two things for self: faith and good actions; and two things for the society: advise each other to truth and advise each other to perseverence.

﴿أَعُوذُ بِاللهِ مِنَ الشَّيْطٰنِ الرَّجِيمِ﴾ ﴿بِسْمِ اللهِ الرَّحْمٰنِ الرَّحِيمِ﴾

1

﴿١﴾ وَالْعَصْرِ

By the time,

➤ The letter وَ means: (1) and; (2) by (oath).

➤ Many Surahs in the Qur'an begin with similar oaths, such as وَالْفَجْرِ، وَالشَّمْسِ، وَاللَّيْلِ.

➤ Allah has taken an oath by time. Time is a witness to what is being said after this oath.

		65	1534
﴿٢﴾ خُسْرٍ	لَفِي	الْإِنْسَانَ	إِنَّ
Loss	**(is) surely in**	**mankind**	**indeed**
	فِي | لَ	إِنْسَان: man	Best example:
	in | surely	الْإِنْسَان: the man, mankind	إِنَّ اللهَ مَعَ الصَّبِرِينَ

➤ In this ayah, we find that in order to show the importance of the subject, Allah began with three distinct forms of emphasis: (1) He took the oath; (2) used إِنَّ; and (3) used لَ.

➤ There is a fourth emphasis in the form of إِلَّا. In a class of 100 students, if 95 fail in the exam, will we say, "All have passed <u>except</u> 95?" No! We say, "All have failed except five." Therefore, the majority of mankind is in loss.

➤ This emphasis after emphasis should increase our attention and force us to think again about what we are doing to avoid loss! Remember the example of Ukasha ﷺ and ask Allah to save us from the loss.

		258	664	
الصّٰلِحٰتِ	وَعَمِلُوا	اٰمَنُوا	الَّذِينَ	إِلَّا
good deeds	**and did**	**have believed**	**those who**	**except**
صَالِح ← صَالِحُوْنَ⁺، صَالِحِينَ⁺	عَمِلُوا | وَ	إِيمَان	صِرَاطَ الَّذِينَ	لَا إِلٰهَ إِلَّا اللهُ
صَالِحَة ← صَالِحَات⁺	they did | and	belief, faith	أَنْعَمْتَ عَلَيْهِمْ	

➤ **Du'aa:** O Allah! Grant me the correct, complete, and firm faith.

➤ **Evaluate:** How is my faith in Allah, the Hereafter, the two angels, the book, the messengers, the fate, and in the Shaitaan that accompanies me throughout the day? Does my faith encourage me to do good things?

➤ What is the state of my faith in Allah's Book? Do I just have the faith or do I care to develop a relationship with it by studying and practising it?

- The Qur'an deals with the details of our beliefs. Reciting the Qur'an with understanding and studying Hadith strengthens and increases our faith.
- Faith alone is not enough to save me from the loss. Good deeds are also essential. What is the quality of my Salah, fasts, Zakah, manners, morals, dealings, etc.?

247

بِالصَّبْرِ 3	وَتَوَاصَوْا	بِالْحَقّ	وَتَوَاصَوْا
to [the] patience.	and advised each other	to the truth,	and advised each other
صَبْر	تَوَاصَوْا | وَ	حَقّ : Truth	تَوَاصَوْا | وَ
perseverance, patience	advised each other | and		advised each other | and

- Good deeds include every good action. Two actions are specially mentioned here: to advise others to the truth and to patience.
- Where will one find the truth? In the Qur'an and in the Sunnah of the Prophet, ﷺ. If we are not able to even understand the Qur'an, then how are we going to propagate the truth to others?
- In many chapters of the Qur'an, Allah describes how the prophets and messengers advised people to the truth, righteousness and patience. Learn from them the way to do it.
- In this ayah, Allah is addressing the people in the plural form! i.e. '*those* who do ...' This shows that we have to work as a team and advise each other to obey Allah in every aspect of our life.
- You can start now by selecting a friend in this class and ask him to be a partner in advising each other to learn the Qur'an and practice it till its completion.
- Patience (Sabr) is of three types: (1) Patience to do good deeds including Da'wah work; (2) patience to stay away from sins; and (3) patience while facing difficulties, diseases, etc.
- When we tell our son or daughter to "Get Educated," we have a detailed plan for his education. Do we have a similar plan for advising people to the righteous path?
- وَ and أَوْ [280]. We need to do four things as mentioned in this Surah because between each task, Allah uses the letter وَ (and). He did not say أَوْ (or).

Lesson 15a	Surah An-Nasr

After completing this lesson (a & b), you will learn **186 new** words, which occur **37,500** times in the Qur'an.

Introduction: According to Abdullah bin Abbas, may Allah be pleased with him, this Surah is the last complete Surah of the Qur'an that was revealed to the Prophet, ﷺ [Muslim, Nasai]. After this Surah, some verses of other Surahs were revealed.

The enemies of Islam were defeated in Arabia and people were accepting Islam in groups because there was no one to scare them or confuse them by telling false things about Islam. They got the freedom to accept it.

اَعُوْذُ بِاللهِ مِنَ الشَّيْطٰنِ الرَّجِيْمِ ۞ بِسْمِ اللهِ الرَّحْمٰنِ الرَّحِيْمِ ۞
171   423

وَالْفَتْحُ [1]	نَصْرُ اللهِ	جَآءَ	اِذَا
and the victory,	the help of Allah	Comes	When
When the help of Allah and the victory comes,			

الْفَتْحُ	وَ	نَصَر: help	جَآءَ: came	إِذْ 239، إِذَا when
victory; opening	and		إِذَا جَآءَ: when (it) comes	

➤ With Allah's help only, things get done.
➤ The victory here refers to the Conquest of Makkah in the 8th year of Hijrah.
➤ **Ask**: O Allah! Grant us your help in everything we do.
➤ **Evaluate**: It took 23 years of hardwork and complete devotion to Allah after which Allah's help came.
➤ **Plan**: What can I do today, this week, or at this stage in my life? One must make an individual and a collective plan so that we also receive the help of Allah. One should spend his money, his time, his resources and his abilities to serve the Deen of Islam. If you are a student, then do your best to excel in studies so you serve Islam the best way.

241

اَفْوَاجًا [2]	فِىْ دِيْنِ اللهِ	يَدْخُلُوْنَ	النَّاسَ	وَرَاَيْتَ
in crowds,	[into] the religion of Allah	entering	the people	and you see

فَوْج: crowd	اللهِ	دِيْن	فِىْ	entry دُخُوْل	إِنْسَان: man	رَاَيْتَ	وَ
أَفْوَاج: crowds	Allah	religion	into	exit خُرُوْج	نَاس: people	you saw	and

➤ Here 'the people' refers to the different tribes of Arabia who entered Islam after the conquest of Makkah.
➤ There are two meanings of Deen: (1) Judgment (2) System of life. Here Deen refers to the system of life. People entering the Deen means that they have become Muslims.
➤ According to the above verse, what is the result of victory and help from Allah? People getting guidance and entering the fold of Islam. Are we helping others to understand Islam so that they can get the best of this world and the Hereafter?

فَسَبّحْ	بِحَمْدِ	رَبّكَ	وَاسْتَغْفِرْهُ
then glorify	with (the) praise	(of) your Lord	and ask forgiveness of Him.
ف	سَبّحْ	ب	حَمْدِ	Who takes care of us and helps us grow	وَ	اسْتَغْفِرْ	هُ
then	glorify	with	Praise		and	ask forgiveness of	Him

➤ سَبّحْ: Say Subhanallah. It means that Allah is free from any defect, deficiency, or imperfection. He does not need anybody's help. He is not weak and He is not under pressure of anyone. He has no son or father. He is alone in His entity, His attributes, His rights and His powers. Refer to lesson No. 7 for the message of Tasbeeh.

➤ فَسَبّحْ بِحَمْدِ How can you praise someone against whom you have a complaint, however small it may be? It is for this reason that we often see the words Alhamdulillah mentioned after Subhanallah.

➤ O Allah! Whatever defect was there in our good deeds, please forgive us for that.

➤ Our Tasbeeh and Hamd are defective. For that also, we should consistently ask His forgiveness. Whenever we get the opportunity to perform a good deed, we should immediately do Tasbeeh, Hamd and ask for forgiveness.

تَوَّابًا 3	كَانَ	إِنَّهُ
Oft-forgiving.	is	Indeed, He
تَابَ: he turned تَائِب: one who turns تَوَّاب: one who turns often تَوَّاب←تَوَّابُونَ⁺ ، تَوَّابِينَ⁺	The regular meaning of كَانَ:was For Allah, كَانَ here means: **is.**	إِنَّ: إِنَّ اللهَ مَعَ الصَّابِرِينَ <u>Indeed</u> Allah is with those who are patient

➤ This is a very big sign of relief and good news for sinners like us. We should never lose hope in the Mercy of Allah. Repent sincerely, i.e., accept that you sinned, feel sorry, and have a firm intention of never repeating the sin. Always have firm belief that Allah will accept your repentance.

➤ **Example**: If I am very hungry and if someone tells me that he feeds hundreds of people, won't I immediately ask him for food. Likewise, in this verse, Allah talks about His immense forgiveness. So one must immediately use the opportunity and ask Allah for forgiveness. Similarly, whenever Allah's name or His act is mentioned, we can use that to ask Allah in a way that benefits us.

Lesson 16a — **Surah Al-Kafiroon**

After completing this lesson (a & b), you will learn **194 new** words, which occur **38,531** times in the Qur'an.

When the polytheists of Makkah saw that more and more people were leaving their religion and reverting to Islam, they came up with an offer of compromise. They told the Prophet ﷺ that they would worship Allah alone for one year but in the following year, the Prophet ﷺ had to worship their gods too along with Allah. In response, Allah revealed this Surah.

The Surah contains a very important message. It tells us that there can be no compromise in the matters of faith.

- The Prophet ﷺ used to recite this Surah and Surah Al-Ikhlaas in the Sunnah Salahs of Fajr and Maghrib. [Musnad Ahmad, Tirmidhi, Nasai, and Ibn Majah].
- The Prophet ﷺ advised some of his companions to recite it before sleep: Recite Surah Al-Kafiroon for it is a clearance from Shirk (associating partners with Allah)." [Abu Dawood].

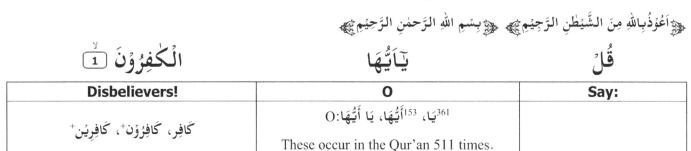

أَعُوْذُبِاللهِ مِنَ الشَّيْطٰنِ الرَّجِيْمِ ﴿ بِسْمِ اللهِ الرَّحْمٰنِ الرَّحِيْمِ ﴾

الْكٰفِرُوْنَ ١	يَآأَيُّهَا	قُلْ
Disbelievers!	O	Say:
كَافِر، كَافِرُوْنَ⁺، كَافِرِيْنَ⁺	361يَا، 153أَيُّهَا، يَا أَيُّهَا:O These occur in the Qur'an 511 times.	

➤ The word يَا occurs in the Qur'an extensively. For example 383يَا قَوْمِ (O people!).
➤ Kafir is the one who receives the message of Islam, understands it, and then rejects it. The general address for Muslims and non-Muslims in the Qur'an is يَا أَيُّهَا النَّاس (O Mankind!).
➤ Here, Allah is very angry at those who came to the Prophet ﷺ to invite him to do Shirk. They had clearly rejected Islam and that's why they are called Kafirs.
➤ The word Kafir itself is not degrading. Allah has asked Muslims to do Kufr with Taghoot (Shaitaan). In that sense, every Muslim has to be a Kafir of Taghoot.
➤ What was the real problem with the disbelievers? They rejected the truth even after recognizing it because of their desires, ego, wealth, status, and traditions.
➤ **Du'aa:** O Allah! Let me not reject the truth because of my ego, desires, or status.
➤ **Evaluate:** How many times did I reject the truth or didn't accept it instantly?
➤ **Plan** to repent. Plan to realize the greatness of Allah and to train oneself to follow the truth.
➤ **Propagate**: Create awareness among people regarding the dangerous consequences of following one's ego and traditions.

تَعْبُدُوْنَ ٢	مَا	لَآ اَعْبُدُ
you worship;	What	I do not worship
تَفْعَلُوْنَ : you all do		أَشْهَدُ : I bear witness; أَعُوْذُ : I take refuge

Ibadah has three meanings: (1) worship; (2) obedience; and (3) slavery. There is no compromise in any of these three. All these are for Allah alone.

> Today, some non-Muslims are trying to defame Islam. In this environment, you have to follow Islam without any inferiority complex. You have to be firm in your belief and thank Allah for Islam and keep spreading the true message of Islam in the best way because many people do not know the truth.

اَعۡبُدُ ﴿3﴾	مَآ	عٰبِدُوۡنَ	وَلَآ اَنۡتُمۡ
I worship;	**(of) what**	**Worshippers**	**and nor are you**
اَشۡهَدُ :I bear witness		عَابِد ، عَابِدُوۡنَ⁺ ، عَابِدِيۡنَ⁺	اَنۡتُمۡ / لَا / وَ
اَعُوۡذُ :I take refuge			you / not / and

> A worship mixed with Shirk is not a worship. Such people are not true worshippers of Allah.
> All religions are not equal. Allah had sent the message to every nation but they lost the original or left it. We should try to present Islam in the best and wise way.

عَبَدتُّمۡ ﴿4﴾	مَّا	عَابِدٌ	وَلَآ اَنَا
you worshipped;	**(of) what**	**(be) a worshipper**	**and nor (will) I**
فَعَلۡتُمۡ :you all did		فَاعِل: doer	اَنَا / لَا / و
عَبَدتُّمۡ :you all worshipped		عَابِد: worshipper	I / not / And

This appears to be a repetition but it is not. There are different messages in the two verses.

> I don't worship your idols now (لَا اَعۡبُدُ) and I will not worship them in future (وَلَآ اَنَا عَابِد).
> I don't worship your present idols (مَا تَعۡبُدُوۡنَ) and I will not worship your past idols (مَا عَبَدتُّمۡ).
> There is no compromise in the matter of faith. It is not because of arrogance but because we follow the truth and we are afraid of Allah's wrath.

اَعۡبُدُ ﴿5﴾	مَآ	عٰبِدُوۡنَ	وَلَآ اَنۡتُمۡ
I worship.	**(of) what**	**Worshippers**	**and nor are you**

> This again appears to be a repetition but it is in a different context. The message here is: Because of your insistence on Shirk, it is not expected that you will worship Allah alone.

دِيۡنِ ﴿6﴾	وَلِىَ	دِيۡنُكُمۡ	لَكُمۡ
my religion.	**and to me**	**your religion**	**To you (be)**

> This does not mean that all religions are equal or same. This also does not mean that we should stop propagating the message of Islam. Did Prophet Muhammad ﷺ stop propagating Islam after this revelation? Never! This statement is in response to their offer of compromise.
> The disbelievers came to the Prophet ﷺ as a team. We should also help each other and work in an organized way to present Islam to the people in the best way so that they are saved from hellfire and get the best of this world and the Hereafter.

Lesson **17a** Purpose of Revelation

After completing this lesson (a & b), you will learn **208 new** words, which occur **39,571** times in the Qur'an.

Introduction: In this lesson, we will study verse 29 of Surah Saad which tells us about the purpose of revelation of the Qur'an very clearly.

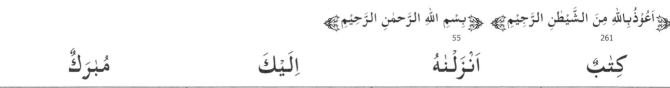

۞ اَعُوْذُبِاللهِ مِنَ الشَّيْطٰنِ الرَّجِيْمِ ۞   ۞ بِسْمِ اللهِ الرَّحْمٰنِ الرَّحِيْمِ ۞

261	55			
كِتٰبٌ	اَنْزَلْنٰهُ		اِلَيْكَ	مُبٰرَكٌ
(It is) a book	We have revealed it		to you (O Muhammad! ﷺ),	full of blessings;
كُتُب + books	اَنْزَلْنَا	هُ	اِلَى	كَ	We say عيد مبارك (Let this Eid be
	We sent down	it	to	you	a blessing for you)

➤ The Qur'an is the book of Allah which is sent down from heavens through Jibra'eel (A).
➤ Allah has already stated that this is a blessed book. But the reason for its revelation is expressed next. If we want to earn the blessings of this book then we have to carry out those things for which it was revealed.
➤ Barakah means to receive a blessing, to have it stay with you, and to have increase in it.
➤ **Qur'an is Mubarak:** The night in which it was revealed became better than 1000 months. So imagine how great the Qur'an is. The month in which it was revealed became the best.
➤ The messenger on which it was revealed became the top messenger. The city in which it was revealed became the city of peace. This book has changed the history of the world. The Sahabah who received this book became the leaders of this world within 100 years. For almost 1000 years, i.e., till the time the Muslims were attached properly to the Qur'an, Muslims retained the leadership in all spheres of life.
➤ We should be extremely happy and say: O Allah! Thank you so much! You are so nice and so caring that You sent us a book full of barakah.
➤ The best use of a blessing is to benefit from it. Therefore, We should recite, understand, ponder, memorize, and spread the Qur'an!
➤ The book is full of barakah. But why did Allah send it down? It is mentioned in the next part. In other words, if we want to receive barakah, we should do those two things.

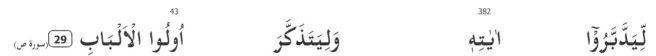

	43					382		
(سورة ص) 29 أُولُوا الْأَلْبَابِ		وَلِيَتَذَكَّرَ		اٰيٰتِهٖ		لِّيَدَّبَّرُوْا	
those of understanding. **and so that those of understanding receive admonition.**		and so that receive admonition			its verses		so that they ponder	
اَلْبَاب	أُولُوا، أُولِي	يَتَذَكَّرَ	لِ	وَ	هٖ	اٰيٰت	يَدَّبَّرُوْا	لِ
understanding	those of	they receive admonition	so that	and	its	verses	they ponder	so that
لُبّ :Intellect اَلْبَاب +				آيَة :sign; verse آيَات +		تَدَبُّر :pondering	

➤ The Qur'an is sent down for: (1) pondering; and (2) taking lessons from it.
➤ Pondering means to think over or reflect upon. You don't need to ponder while reading a newspaper. Reading it once is enough to get the message. But can you read a book of science, math, or commerce in the same way? No! You have to stop and think over or ponder.
➤ If we realize the greatness of the book, we will be more motivated to ponder it. This book is sent by the Creator of this universe who was always there and will always be there; whose universe is so big that just

to go out of our own galaxy, we will need 100,000 years if we travel at the speed of light (3,00,000 kilometers/sec). Allah sent it down from above the seven heavens.

➢ To ponder the Qur'an or reflect upon it, you have to understand it first!
➢ Receiving admonition means to take lessons, to listen the advice, to implement them in our lives. For example, if you tell a student, "Prepare for the exams, otherwise you will fail." If he prepares for the exam then he has acted on your advice.
➢ You can do so by acting upon its commandments and staying away from its prohibitions.
➢ When we do the above two, then by Allah's Will, we can earn all the blessings of this world and the Hereafter through the Qur'an.

Our relationship with the Qur'an:

1 **Direct:** The Qur'an is Allah's word. Whenever I hear it or recite it, I should **feel** that Allah is directly addressing me. He sees me how I react to His words!

2 **Personal:** Every verse of the Qur'an is for me. Let us not say that this verse is for kaafir, mushrik, or munafiq. I have to see what is there in it for me! Why did Allah address this to me?

3 **Planned:** Every grain is destined for someone to eat! In the same manner, each and every verse is destined for someone to hear or recite. If I heard Surah Qaaf in Fajr today, then it has something to do with what I am doing today.

4 **Relevant:** Qur'an is a reminder. Can Allah's reminder be irrelevant? I should ask O Allah! Why did you make me hear or recite this verse(s) today?

Tadabbur تَدَبُّر: It means thinking over or pondering. Below is a simple method of Tadabbur for a common man. There are many aspects of Tadabbur but we are talking about basics only.

- Study: Study the verses repeatedly with understanding. Study brief commentary or Tafseer if available.
- Visualize: Use your imagination to visualize what is stated there. For example, when Allah talks about the heavens or the earth, try to visualize them.
- Feel: Recite with feelings. For Example, recite the ayah about Jannah with hope and about hell with fear.

Tadhakkur تَذَكُّر: It means taking lessons or receiving admonition. Following is a simple method to do it.

- Ask: Extract a du'aa from the passage you have learnt and ask Allah to help you implement what you are asking. For example, for the verse of this lesson: O Allah help me do Tadabbur. Just Du'aa is not enough. One should evaluate his performance and make plans. Otherwise it will be like a student who prays to Allah in Fajr, Zuhr, Asr, etc. to help him pass the exams but he does not go to school nor studies any book!
- Evaluate: What have you done so far regarding the work related to Du'aa. For example, how much time did I invest last day in Tadabbur? If you did, alhamdulillah; if not, astaghfirullah.
- Plan: What is the plan regarding the work related to Du'aa. For example, how much time will you give for Tadabbur every day?

Regarding the plan, we have to be careful and check one thing: When it comes to group or Fiqh issues or any new idea, then please check with scholars before you mention it to others or implement it.

For common people like us, there are many areas that we can work on such as: Relationship with Allah, obeying the Prophet ﷺ, planning for the Hereafter, different types of worship, morals, good dealings, dawah, ordering good and stopping evil, team spirit, etc.

Tableegh (Conveying): The Prophet ﷺ said,

بَلِّغُوْا	عَنِّيْ	وَلَوْ	اٰیَةً
Convey	from me	even if	(it is a single) verse.

It means whatever we are reading from the Quran and Hadith, we have to convey it to others. Try to convey the beautiful Message of Islam to others in the best possible way.

We have to invest our time, money, and abilities in this task and help those who are working in the Da'wah field.

The logo shown here is placed at the beginning of every lesson to remind you about the basics of Tadabbur, Tazakkur, and Tableegh.

To do Tadabbur and Tadhakkur on every Ayah or Dhikr , we can use this logo: Study it, ponder it, visualize it, and feel it.

- ➤ Ask Allah according to the topic of the Ayah
- ➤ Evaluate your past in the light of this Du'aa
- ➤ Plan for the upcoming days
- ➤ Propagate the message so that we can fulfil our responsibility and get reward too.

Based on verses like this, the scholars have listed the rights of the Qur'an as follows: Believe in it, read it, understand it, ponder its verses, act upon it, spread it, etc.

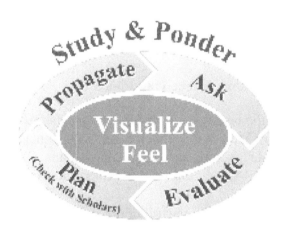

Lesson 18a — Qu'ran is Easy to Learn

After completing this lesson (a & b), you will learn **222 new** words, which occur **40,469** times in the Qur'an.

In the last lesson, we have learnt that Allah has revealed the Qur'an for pondering and acting upon it. To ponder its verses, i.e., Arabic verses because the Qur'an cannot be translated.

Somebody may say that this is a blind belief. It is not! For example, take a couplet of the best poetry in your language (if it is not English) and try to translate into English. You can't! The beauty, the power, the balance, the depth, selection of recurring and matching words, … everything is gone! If human composition cannot be translated, how can Allah's 'composition' be translated?

This means even if you have read 100 translations of the Holy Qur'an, in simple terms you have not read it at all! The Qur'an is Arabic Qur'an only! Please note that We are not negating the rewards (10 rewards for each letter recited) and not decreasing the value of translation because we will learn Arabic through the translation only. The point is: Translation is not our destination.

The Arabic Qur'an has a "Spiritual voltage" that penetrates deep into the heart because it is Allah's book. There are many spiritual effects of the verses and Surahs. You get 10 rewards for reciting each letter of the Arabic Qur'an.

The verses of the Qur'an are in Arabic and the Qur'an cannot be translated. We can get only the message of the Qur'an in the translation. To ponder the Arabic verses, we have to learn Arabic.

It is a huge blessing from Allah that He has made the Qur'an easy to understand. Its Arabic is also easy to learn as far as basic understanding is concerned.

اَعُوْذُبِاللهِ مِنَ الشَّيْطٰنِ الرَّجِيْمِ بِسْمِ اللهِ الرَّحْمٰنِ الرَّحِيْمِ

لِلذِّكْرِ (القَمَر: 17)	الْقُرْاٰنَ	يَسَّرْنَا	وَلَقَدْ
to understand and remember	**the Qur'an**	**We have made easy**	**And indeed**

الذِّكْر	لِ		يُسْر: easy	قَدْ	لَ	وَ
understand & remember	for, to	The meaning of the Qur'an is "one which is recited often."	عُسْر: difficult	Already	indeed	and
ذِكْر has two meanings: (1) to memorize; and (2) to understand and take lessons			يَسَّرْنَا: we made easy	قَدْ قَامَتِ الصَّلٰوة Salah is already established.		

➤ The word Qur'an means that which is read often. Even its name has miracle in it. Indeed, according to even non-Muslims, Qur'an is "the most widely read book in existence" [Encyclopedia Britannica].

➤ Qur'an is easy for learning, practicing, and for advising others too. Understand it well so that you learn its style, arguments, stories, and proofs thoroughly.

➤ Never ever think, say, or accept that the Qur'an is difficult to understand. Are we going to contradict this verse? May Allah forgive us.

➤ Qur'an is easy to learn, but it is not automatic. You have to spend time and effort for learning it. The Prophet ﷺ said that Allah runs towards the one who walks towards Him. Let us start walking first and you will be amazed to see the results.

➤ Qur'an is easy to understand and take lessons from it. It is easy to see what Allah wants me to believe and to practice.

➤ Please don't mix it with Fiqh or legal issues. For that, we should ask scholars.

Let us take a Hadith now.

خَيْرُكُم	مَنْ	تَعَلَّمَ الْقُرْاٰنَ	وَعَلَّمَهُ (بخارى)
The best of you	**(is the one) who**	**learns the Qur'an**	**and teaches it.**
خَيْرٌ good, best	كُمْ your	First question in the grave: مَنْ رَبُّكَ؟ Who is your Rabb?	تَعَلَّمَ: learnt	عَلَّمَ: taught	وَ and	عَلَّمَ taught	هُ It

> The Prophet ﷺ mentioned the student first and then the teacher. This is a great honor for every student of the Qur'an. It also means that there is no end to learning the Book of Allah! Hence, we should keep learning more and more about it till we die.
> It also means that the best person is the one who does both the learning and the teaching.
> Whatever we have learnt so far is very easy to teach. Can you write at least 2 names whom you will teach.
> Right now, millions of classes may be running on the earth. The best in the sight of Allah are those where the Qur'an is taught.
> Till now, you may have attended thousands of classes but this class or a similar Qur'an class is the most valuable in the sight of Allah because we are learning the Qur'an.
> Learning the Qur'an does not mean just learning how to read it. It also means how to understand it, ponder it, implement it, etc.
> The Prophet ﷺ was sent as a teacher of the Qur'an. He taught the Qur'an by explaining it and practicing it. To learn the way the Sahabah (the companions of the Prophet ﷺ learnt, first we have to learn how to read Arabic letters and words along with Tajweed. Don't stop there because the real learning of the Qur'an starts after it, i.e., how to understand it and practice it.

Let us take another Hadith:

بِالنِّيَّاتِ (بخارى)	[41] [145] إِنَّمَا الْأَعْمَالُ
on intentions.	**Actions (are based) only**
نِيَّة intention	نِيَّات⁺ intentions	إِنَّمَا: only عَمَل، أَعْمَال⁺

> On the Day of Judgment, the case of three people will be decided first. Among them will be a reciter of the Qur'an who used to recite to show-off. He will be thrown into the hell because of his wrong intention. Allah doesn't accept those deeds which are done to show others along with Him.
> Let us learn the Qur'an to please Allah only. Learn it to understand and practice it.
> Let us learn it to teach others for the sake of Allah because a huge majority is away from the Qur'an. Perhaps 90% of Non-Arab Muslims today do not understand the Qur'an. If we teach them the Qur'an, they will be able to convey it to others.

The three words given in the table below occur **2370 times** in the Qur'an. Remember their meanings by using the following examples. It is easier to remember and recall the meanings if you remember their examples too. The examples are very useful, especially when you get confused and start mixing the meaning of one with the other similar sound word (such as إِنْ and إِنَّ).

If Allah wills	إِنْ [56] شَاءَ الله	If	إِنْ [691]
Indeed Allah is with those who are patient	إِنَّ الله مَعَ الصّٰبِرِينَ	Indeed	إِنَّ [1534]
Actions are (based) **only** on intentions	إِنَّمَا الْأَعْمَالُ بِالنِّيَّاتِ	Only	إِنَّمَا [145]

After completing this lesson (a & b), you will learn **232 new** words, which occur 41,111 times in the Qur'an.

Introduction: In this lesson, we will learn the best ways to learn the Qur'an: (1) Ask Allah for knowledge; (2) Use all the resources starting with the pen; and (3) Try to compete and excel.

❶ Ask Allah for knowledge

عِلْمًا 114 (سورة طه)	زِدْنِيْ	رَبِّ
in knowledge.	**Increase me**	**O, My Lord!**

عِلْم: knowledge	نِيْ	زِدْ	رَبّ: Takes care of us & helps us grow
	me	increase	

➢ Allah taught this Du'aa (supplication) to Prophet ﷺ especially for memorizing and learning the Qur'an. We should, therefore, beg Allah using this Du'aa repeatedly and sincerely.

➢ Tip to remind us to receipt this Duaa: You may link it to the word 'ilm' in Ayatul-Kursi and after you recite ayatal kursi or after Adhkaar, say: رَبِّ زِدْنِيْ عِلْمًا

➢ Along with Du'aa, we must make a plan and spend time every day to understand the Qur'an. If a student asks Allah for success in every Salah but does not go to school nor open any book to study, will he pass the exam? If we just pray for knowledge but don't make an effort then we are playing with the Du'aa?

➢ Some people say that you don't need to know more; just practice what you know. This statement is not correct. The only Du'aa taught by Allah for increase is the increase in knowledge! More knowledge will give us stronger faith and then it will be easier to obey Allah. It will also help us spread it in a better way. It will be easier to understand and avoid the attacks of Shaitaan.

➢ How should you pray? Like a person who is hungry for two or three days; Like a heart patient who will undergo an open heart surgery the next day. Will he ask Allah only once? Will he ask without feelings? Ask Allah again and again to help us understand every page of the most important book of knowledge.

❷ Use all the resources starting with the pen

304

بِالْقَلَمِ 4 (سورة العلق)	عَلَّمَ	اَلَّذِيْ
by the pen.	**taught**	**(The one) Who**

الْقَلَم	بِ	تَعَلَّمَ: learnt	الَّذِيْ: the one who
pen	by	عَلَّمَ: taught	الَّذِيْنَ: those who

➢ When Allah says that He taught by the pen, pick up the pen immediately! You have written millions of words with your hand. Now use your hand for learning Qura'nic Arabic and make it a habit.

➢ Where will you write? Maintain a notebook. Keep a record of what you are learning. Develop a small library of books and notebooks.

➢ According to modern research, writing helps you learn things effectively. You have to first read or listen to things, think about it, and then use your eyes and fingers to write while keeping the whole body silent and focused on the task.

- Make a vow to yourself today that you will spare at least five minutes for writing the meanings and the grammatical forms of new words. Do it not with laziness but with passion, devotion, and sincerity.
- If there is any knowledge that this Ummah is deficient in, it is the knowledge of the Qur'an, whose first word of the first revelation is, "Read!" اِقْرَأْ. Make reading and writing your special habit especially when it comes to learning the Qur'an.

③ Compete and try to excel

عَمَلًا (الْمُلْك: 2)		36 اَحْسَنُ			59 اَيُّكُمْ	
in deeds?			**is best**		**Which of you**	
عَمَل، أَعْمَال		أَكْبَر	كَبِير	Big	كُمْ	اَيُّ
		أَصْغَر	صَغِير	Small	your, you	which of
		أَحْسَن	حَسَن	Good		

- Allah created us not just to see who is a Muslim and who is not; but to see who is best. Best in individual works, i.e., best in praying; best in homes; best in office, etc.. best in social works such as helping others, doing Da'wah, enjoining good, and forbidding evil.
- You have started learning the Qur'an. Allah is watching us right now to see who is better in learning the Qur'an in this class? Only for the sake of Allah, try to be better than others. Allah will reward you based on your efforts. Just try your best and compete.
- Shaitaan is burning in rage. Why? Because you have taken the first step towards learning the Qur'an. He will try his level best to stop you. Shaitaan is very experienced but you enjoy the support of Allah.
- Shaitaan is ready, angels are also ready, their pens are also ready to record your deeds. Are you ready?

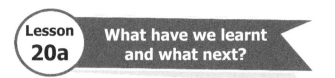

After completing this lesson (a & b), you will learn **232 new** words, which occur 41,111 times in the Qur'an.

Introduction: In this lesson, we will pick two selections from the Qur'an to show how much we have learnt in this course.

1. The first five verses of Surah Al-Baqarah

The underlined words are those that you have already learnt in this course. As you can see, in the past 19 lessons, you have learnt more than 50% words of these verses, Alhamdulillah.

الٓمّ ١	ذٰلِكَ	الْكِتٰبُ	لَا رَيْبَ	فِيهِ	هُدًى	لِّلْمُتَّقِينَ ٢
Alif Laam Meem.	That	is the Book.	No doubt	in it,	a guidance	for the God-conscious

الَّذِينَ	يُؤْمِنُونَ	بِالْغَيْبِ	وَيُقِيمُونَ	الصَّلٰوةَ	وَمِمَّا	رَزَقْنٰهُمْ
Those who	Believe	in the unseen	and establish	the prayer	and out of what	We have provided Them

وَالَّذِينَ ٣	يُؤْمِنُونَ	بِمَآ	أُنْزِلَ	اِلَيْكَ	وَمَآ
they spend.	And those who	believe	in what	is sent down	to you	and what

أُنْزِلَ	مِنْ قَبْلِكَ	وَبِالْاٰخِرَةِ	هُمْ	يُوقِنُونَ ٤
was sent down	before you	and in the Hereafter	they	firmly believe.

أُولٰٓئِكَ	عَلٰى	هُدًى	مِّنْ	رَّبِّهِمْ
Those	are on	guidance	from	their Lord

وَأُولٰٓئِكَ	هُمْ	الْمُفْلِحُونَ ٥
and those,	they	are the successful ones.

2. Ayat Al-Kursi (Verse 255 of Al-Baqarah)

The underlined words are those that you have already learnt in this course. As you can see, in the past 19 lessons, you have learnt more than 50% words of these verses, Alhamdulillah.

الْقَيُّومُ	اَلْحَيُّ	هُوَ	اِلَّا	اِلٰهَ	لَا	اَللّٰهُ
the Sustainer and Protector (of all that exists).	the Ever-Living	He,	but	God	No	Allah,

نَوْمٌ	وَّلَا	سِنَةٌ	لَا تَأْخُذُهُ
sleep.	and not	slumber	Does not overtake Him

فِى الْأَرْضِ	وَمَا	فِى السَّمٰوٰتِ	مَا	لَهُ
on the earth.	and whatever is	in the heavens	whatever is	To Him belongs

بِاِذْنِهٖ	اِلَّا	عِنْدَهٗ	يَشْفَعُ	ذَا الَّذِىْ	مَنْ
with His permission?	except	with Him	can intercede	is he that	Who

خَلْفَهُمْ	وَمَا	بَيْنَ اَيْدِيْهِمْ	مَا	يَعْلَمُ
behind them;	and that which is	before them	that which is	He knows

بِمَا شَاءَ	اِلَّا	مِّنْ عِلْمِهٖ	بِشَىْءٍ	وَلَا يُحِيْطُوْنَ
that which He wills	except	of His knowledge	anything	and they will never encompass

وَالْاَرْضَ	السَّمٰوٰتِ	كُرْسِيُّهُ	وَسِعَ
and the earth.	the heavens	His chair encompasses	

الْعَظِيْمُ	الْعَلِىُّ	وَهُوَ	حِفْظُهُمَا	وَلَا يَئُوْدُهٗ
the Most Great.	is the Most High,	And He	the guarding and preserving both of them.	And does not tire Him

Arabic
Grammar

Lesson 1b — هُوَ، هُمْ، أَنْتَ، أَنَا، أَنْتُمْ، نَحْنُ

After completing this lesson (a & b), you will learn **12 new** words, which occur **7,248** times in the Qur'an.

GRAMMAR:

In this lesson, we will learn 6 words: نَحْنُ، أَنْتُمْ، أَنَا، أَنْتَ، هُمْ، هُوَ. These six words occur **1295 times** in the Qur'an! Learn these words using TPI (Total Physical Interaction), i.e., using all your senses. You hear it, see it, think it, say it, and show it. Make sure that you do this practice with full attention and love.

❶ When you say هُوَ (he), point the index finger of the right hand towards your right as if that person is sitting on your right. When you say هُمْ (they), point four fingers of your right hand towards your right. In a class, both the teacher and the student should practice this together.

❷ When you say أَنْتَ (you), point the index finger of your right hand to someone sitting in front of you. When you say أَنَا (I), point the index finger of your right hand towards yourself.

❸ When you say أَنْتُمْ (you all), point four fingers of your right hand to the front. When you say نَحْنُ (we) point the four fingers of your right hand towards yourself.

Guidelines for Practice: Make sure to learn two forms at a time to make it easy. For the first 3 times, practice these forms with translation, i.e., just show and say هُوَ he, هُمْ they. Since you will be showing what you mean by your hand, you don't need to translate each of them after 3 cycles. Just say it in Arabic, i.e., هُوَ، هُمْ. This is the immediate benefit of using TPI, among many others.

Continue the above steps without translating these words. After the first pair is learnt thoroughly, go for the next two, and so on. Just a few minutes of your practice using TPI will make the learning of these six words extremely easy!!!

At this point, don't worry about learning the terminologies (first person, singular, pronoun etc.). Just focus on these six words and their meanings. After learning the six words, you can practice spoken Arabic using the sentences given below. Note that مَنْ means who.

❀❀❀**Spoken Arabic**❀❀❀

He, They...	
He	هُوَ [481]
They	هُمْ [444]
You	أَنْتَ [81]
I	أَنَا [68]
you all	أَنْتُمْ [135]
We	نَحْنُ [86]

Interestingly, commonly occurring words are joined with others in Arabic. For example: وَ: and; فَ: thus.
Let us take the first two words from the table above. In that case:

وَهُوَ: and he; وَهُمْ: and they; فَهُوَ: thus he; فَهُمْ: thus they

In a similar way, you can join وَ and فَ with other words too.

Below the spoken-Arabic heading, the following Arabic sentences appear (read right to left):

مَنْ هُوَ؟ [831]   هُوَ مُسْلِم

مَنْ هُمْ؟   هُمْ مُسْلِمُون

مَنْ أَنْتَ؟

أَنَا مُسْلِم

مَنْ أَنْتُمْ؟

نَحْنُ مُسْلِمُون

www.understandquran.com   54

Lesson 2b

هُوَ مُسْلِمٌ، هُمْ مُسْلِمُونَ...

After completing this lesson (a & b), you will learn **27 new** words, which occur **8,638** times in the Qur'an.

GRAMMAR: In Arabic, a word can be of one of the three types. The first is إِسْم

1. إِسْم (Noun): It can be a name (Ex: كِتَابٌ) or an attribute (Ex: مُسْلِم، مُسْلِمُونَ).

Common noun and proper Noun: When the noun is referring to a specific person or thing, then لْ is added before the noun. Since Arabic words don't start with Sukoon letters, we add a temporary Hamzah there and say: اَلْ

the Muslim	الْمُسْلِمُ	a Muslim	مُسْلِمٌ 42
the believer	الْمُؤْمِنُ	a believer	مُؤْمِنٌ 230
the pious person	الصَّالِحُ	a pious person	صَالِحٌ 136
the disbeliever	الْكَافِرُ	a disbeliever	كَافِرٌ 134
the polytheist	الْمُشْرِكُ	a polytheist	مُشْرِكٌ 49

Making Plurals: Let us take some nouns and learn how to make their plurals. Every language has its own way of making plurals. In English, we add "s" to a singular noun to make it plural. In Arabic, a plural is formed by adding ون or ين at the end of a word. There are other rules too for making plurals. We will learn them later, InshaAllah.

Let us practice the following at least three times:

Plural		Singular
مُسْلِمُوْن، مُسْلِمِيْن	←	مُسْلِم
مُؤْمِنُوْن، مُؤْمِنِيْن	←	مُؤْمِن
صَالِحُوْن، صَالِحِيْن	←	صَالِح
كَافِرُوْن، كَافِرِيْن	←	كَافِر
مُشْرِكُوْن، مُشْرِكِيْن	←	مُشْرِك

Signs for Nouns: They start with اَلْ or end with ـَة، ـٍ، ـٌ، ـيْنَ، ـُوْنَ، ات etc.

Let us apply these rules to what we have learnt in the last lesson, i.e., هُوَ، هُمْ، أَنْتَ، أَنْتُمْ، أَنَا، نَحْنُ.

✧✧✧ Spoken Arabic ✧✧✧

٩٣ هَلْ هُوَ مُسْلِم؟   ٤ نَعَمْ، هُوَ مُسْلِم

هَلْ هُمْ مُسْلِمُونَ؟   نَعَمْ، هُمْ مُسْلِمُونَ

هَلْ أَنْتَ مُسْلِم؟

نَعَمْ، أَنَا مُسْلِم

هَلْ أَنْتُمْ مُسْلِمُونَ؟

نَعَمْ، نَحْنُ مُسْلِمُونَ

Pronouns (with examples)	
He is a Muslim.	هُوَ مُسْلِم
They are Muslims.	هُمْ مُسْلِمُونَ
You are a Muslim.	أَنْتَ مُسْلِم
I am a Muslim.	أَنَا مُسْلِم
You are Muslims.	أَنْتُمْ مُسْلِمُونَ
We are Muslims.	نَحْنُ مُسْلِمُونَ

For the first 3 times, repeat each sentence in the table along with its translation, i.e., show and say هُوَ مُسْلِم He is a Muslim; هُمْ مُسْلِمُونَ They are Muslims; etc. For the next 3 cycles, just repeat Arabic sentences using TPI, i.e., just say هُوَ مُسْلِم، هُمْ مُسْلِمُونَ etc.

Continue the above steps without translation. Just five minutes of your practice using TPI will make the learning of these six sentences extremely easy!!! After you do that, practice sentences using Spoken Arabic dialogues given above.

Lesson 3b

رَبُّهُ، رَبُّهُمْ ...

After completing this lesson (a & b), you will learn **33 new** words, which occur **12,089** times in the Qur'an.

GRAMMAR: In the last lessons, you learnt the words for *he, they, you, you all, I,* and *we.* In this lesson, we will learn the words for *his, their, your, your, my,* and *our.* In Arabic, these are not independent words; they are suffixed to nouns, verbs, or prepositions. We, therefore, learn these forms by attaching them to a noun رَبّ (Lord; Sustainer and Cherisher; the One who takes care of us and helps us grow). Please note that these attachments occur in the Qur'an almost 8,000 times, i.e., almost once in every line! They are extremely important. Make sure that you practice them thoroughly using TPI.

Make sure to learn two forms at a time to make it easy. After learning the six terms, you can then repeat the whole table.

☆☆☆ Spoken Arabic ☆☆☆		773* رَبّ... + (ـهُ، هُمْ،...)		His, their, your, ...	
رَبُّهُ اللهُ	مَنْ رَبُّهُ؟	His Rabb	رَبُّهُ	His	ـهُ
رَبُّهُمُ اللهُ	مَنْ رَبُّهُمْ؟	Their Rabb	رَبُّهُمْ	Their	هُمْ
	مَنْ رَبُّكَ؟	Your Rabb	رَبُّكَ	Your	ـكَ
رَبِّيَ اللهُ		My Rabb	رَبِّي	My	ـِي
	مَنْ رَبُّكُمْ؟	Your Rabb	رَبُّكُمْ	Your	كُمْ
رَبُّنَا اللهُ		Our Rabb	رَبُّنَا	Our	ـنَا

*We have already taken into count the word رَبّ (199 times) in Lesson No. 2a, therefore the remaining words occurr 772 times in the Qur'an.

Give special attention to كَ، يْ، كُمْ، نَا (your, mine, your, our).

After learning the above words, practice spoken Arabic using the sentences above.

We can also have: دِينُكَ: Your Deen;   دِينِي: My Deen.

Let us take two more dialogues: (مَا [2154] : what)

دِينِي الْإِسْلَامُ   مَا دِينُكَ؟

Lesson
4b

هِيَ، هَا، مُسْلِمَة، مُسْلِمَات

After completing this lesson (a & b),
you will learn **44 new** words, which
occur **15,387** times in the Qur'an.

GRAMMAR:

Let us learn Arabic words for she and her.

[64]هِيَ: she. when you say هِيَ (she) or هَا (her) show towards your left using the pointing of your left hand; as if that lady is on your left side.

To make the feminine gender of most of the nouns, just add ة at the end. For example:

❁❁❁**Spoken Arabic**❁❁❁

هِيَ مُسْلِمَة ← هُوَ مُسْلِم

هِيَ مُؤْمِنَة ← هُوَ مُؤْمِن

هِيَ صَالِحَة ← هُوَ صَالِح

Singular Feminine		Singular Masculine
مُسْلِمَة	←	مُسْلِم
مُؤْمِنَة	←	مُؤْمِن
صَالِحَة	←	صَالِح
صَابِرَة	←	صَابِر
شَاكِرَة	←	شَاكِر

هَا: her. (this word comes always in the last).

Memory tip: After any Sahabi's (companion of the Prophet ﷺ) names, we generally use رَضِيَ الله عَنْهُ (may Allah be pleased with him). Similarly, for a woman of that group, we use رَضِيَ الله عَنْهَا.

For example, أَبُوبَكْر رَضِيَ الله عَنْهُ، عَائِشَة رَضِيَ الله عَنْهَا.

❁❁❁**Spoken Arabic**❁❁❁

مَنْ رَبُّهَا؟ ← رَبُّهَا الله

مَا دِيْنُهَا؟ ← دِيْنُهَا الْإِسْلَام

مَا كِتَابُهَا؟ ← كِتَابُهَا الْقُرْآن

Feminine forms	
her Lord	رَبُّهَا
her way of life	دِيْنُهَا
her book	كِتَابُهَا

Plural Feminine: The rule for making their plurals is to replace ة with ات at the end. There are other rules as well that you will study later.

Plural Feminine		Singular Feminine
مُسْلِمَات	←	مُسْلِمَة
مُؤْمِنَات	←	مُؤْمِنَة
صَالِحَات	←	صَالِحَة

 لِ، مِنْ، عَنْ

After completing this lesson (a & b), you will learn **57 new** words, which occur **19,471** times in the Qur'an.

GRAMMAR: In Arabic, a word can be of one of the three types:

❶ اسْم (Noun): Name (Ex: كِتَاب، مَكَّة) or an attribute (Ex: مُسْلِم، مُؤْمِن)

❷ فِعْل (Verb): Indicates the action (Ex: فَتَحَ، نَصَرُوا)

❸ حَرْف (Letter): Joins nouns and/or verbs (Ex: لَ، مِنْ، عَنْ، مَعَ، إِنَّ)

In previous lessons, we took a few **nouns** and made their plurals. In this lesson, we will learn **letters**: (لَ، مِنْ، عَنْ). These three are prepositions. Learn the meanings along with examples given below. These examples are very useful in remembering the meanings of these letters. In the examples given below.

for : لَ

My religion	and **for** me,	your religion	**For** you
دِيْنِ	وَلِيَ	دِيْنُكُمْ	لَكُمْ

from : مِنْ

the outcast.	from Satan,	in Allah	I seek refuge
الرَّجِيْمِ	مِنَ الشَّيْطٰنِ	بِاللهِ	اَعُوْذُ

with : عَنْ

with him	(May) Allah be pleased
عَنْهُ	رَضِيَ اللهُ

✧✧✧**Spoken Arabic**✧✧✧

The Qur'an is for everyone. Let's start by asking: Is it for him?

نَعَمْ، هٰذَا لَهُ   أَهٰذَا لَهُ؟

نَعَمْ، هٰذَا لَهُمْ   أَهٰذَا لَهُمْ؟

أَهٰذَا لَكَ؟

نَعَمْ، هٰذَا لِيْ

أَهٰذَا لَكُمْ؟

نَعَمْ، هٰذَا لَنَا

for : لَ (اَلْحَمْدُ لِلهِ)	1361
for him	لَهُ
for them	لَهُمْ
for you	لَكَ
for me	لِيْ
for you all	لَكُمْ
for us	لَنَا

from…: مِنْ 744*	
We have already taken into count the word مِنْ (2471 times) in Lesson No.1a, therefore the remaining words occurr 744 times.	
from him	مِنْهُ
from them	مِنْهُمْ
from you	مِنْكَ
from me	مِنِّي
from you all	مِنْكُمْ
from us	مِنَّا

with: عَنْ 416	
with him	عَنْهُ
with them	عَنْهُمْ
with you	عَنْكَ
with me	عَنِّي
with you all	عَنْكُمْ
with us	عَنَّا

Before this, we have learnt رَبُّهُ: his Rabb; رَبُّهَا: her Rabb. Similarly,

لَهُ: for him;   لَهَا: for her

مِنْهُ: from him;   مِنْهَا: from her

عَنْهُ: with him;   عَنْهَا: with her

Lesson 6b   بِ، فِي، عَلَىٰ

After completing this lesson (a & b), you will learn **63 new** words, which occur **23,267** times in the Qur'an.

GRAMMAR: In this lesson, we will learn three more letters: بِ، فِي، عَلَىٰ. These three prepositions occur 3617 times in Quran with 7 Pronouns. Example sentences given below are very useful for remembering the meanings of these letters. In the examples below, Use TPI here and practice them thoroughly.

	بِسْمِ	بِ : in
of Allah	**In** the name	

	فِي سَبِيلِ 176	فِي : in
of Allah	**In** the path	

عَلَيْكُمْ	اَلسَّلَامُ	عَلَىٰ : on
on you	Peace	

The word سُبُل، +سَبِيل (the way) occurs in the Qur'an 176 times.

with, in بِ : 510	
in him	بِهِ
in them	بِهِمْ
in you	بِكَ
in me	بِي
in you all	بِكُمْ
in us	بِنَا

Answer the following questions keeping in mind that Allah has kept something good in all of us.

in : فِي 1684	
in him	فِيهِ
in them	فِيهِم
in you	فِيكَ
in me	فِيَّ
in you all	فِيكُم
in us	فِينَا

هَلْ فِيهِ خَيْرٌ؟   نَعَم، فِيهِ خَيْرٌ

هَلْ فِيهِم خَيْرٌ؟   نَعَم، فِيهِم خَيْرٌ

هَلْ فِيكَ خَيْرٌ؟

نَعَم، فِيَّ خَيْرٌ

هَلْ فِيكُم خَيْرٌ؟

نَعَم، فِينَا خَيْرٌ

on : عَلَى 1207*	
We have already taken into count the word عَلَيهِم (216 times) in Lesson No. 4a, therefore the remaining words occurr 1207 times.	
on him	عَلَيهِ
on them	عَلَيهِم
on you	عَلَيكَ
on me	عَلَيَّ
on you all	عَلَيكُم
on us	عَلَينَا

We have learnt رَبُّهُ: his Rabb; رَبُّهَا: her Rabb. Similarly,

بِهِ: in him;   بِهَا: in her

فِيهِ: in him;   فِيهَا: in her

عَلَيهِ: on him;   عَلَيهَا: on her

Lesson 7b — إلَى، مَعَ، عِنْدَ

After completing this lesson (a & b), you will learn **80 new** words, which occur **26,082** times in the Qur'an.

GRAMMAR: In this lesson, we will learn three more words: إلَى، مَعَ، عِنْدَ These three words occur 1096 times in Quran with 7 Pronouns. Example sentences given below are very useful for remembering the meanings of these words. In the examples below.

رَاجِعُوْنَ،	اِلَيْهِ	وَإِنَّا	لِلّٰهِ	إِنَّا	to, toward : إلَى
will return."	towards Him	and indeed we	belong to Allah	"Indeed, we	

الصَّابِرِيْنَ	مَعَ	اللّٰه	اِنَّ	with : مَعَ
the patient ones.	(is) with	Allah	Indeed	

عِنْدَكَ؟	رِيَالًا	كَمْ	with : عِنْدَ
with you?	Riyals	How many	

✾✾✾ Spoken Arabic ✾✾✾

نَعَمْ عِنْدَهُ قَلَم   هَلْ عِنْدَهُ قَلَم؟

نَعَمْ عِنْدَهُمْ قَلَمْ   هَلْ عِنْدَهُمْ قَلَمْ؟

هَلْ عِنْدَكَ قَلَمْ؟

نَعَمْ عِنْدِي قَلَمْ

هَلْ عِنْدَكُمْ قَلَمْ؟

نَعَمْ عِنْدَنَا قَلَمْ

with : عِنْدَ 197	
with him; near him; he has	عِنْدَهُ
with them; near them; they have	عِنْدَهُمْ
with you; near you; you have	عِنْدَكَ
with me; near me; I have	عِنْدِي
with you all; near you; you have	عِنْدَكُمْ
with us; near us; we have	عِنْدَنَا

to, toward : إِلَى 736	
to him	إِلَيْهِ
to them	إِلَيْهِمْ
to you	إِلَيْكَ
to me	إِلَيَّ
to you all	إِلَيْكُمْ
to us	إِلَيْنَا

with : مَعَ 163	
With him	مَعَهُ
With them	مَعَهُمْ
With you	مَعَكَ
With me	مَعِي
With you all	مَعَكُمْ
With us	مَعَنَا

We have learnt رَبُّهُ: his Rabb; رَبُّهَا: her Rabb. Similarly,

عِنْدَهُ: near him;   عِنْدَهَا: near her

إِلَيْهِ: to him;   إِلَيْهَا: to her

عَلَيْهِ: on him;   عَلَيْهَا: on her

Lesson 8b

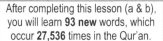
After completing this lesson (a & b), you will learn **93 new** words, which occur **27,536** times in the Qur'an.

GRAMMAR - Three Tips on Prepositions:

You have learnt several prepositions in the last two lessons. Prepositions change their meanings depending upon the context. If you remember the following tips, you will know how to understand them.

❶ The Same thing is expressed in different languages using different prepositions. For example:

اٰمَنْتُ بِاللهِ   I believed in Allah;   (in Urdu) میں اللہ پر ایمان لایا

The above 3 sentences in 3 different languages express the same fact, i.e., I believed, but the preposition in each language is different in its basic meanings (with, in, and on).

❷ For the same language, a preposition may be or may not be required depending upon the verb being used. Example: I <u>said</u> **to** him; I <u>told</u> him.
Sometimes, a preposition may be there in Arabic but not required in English (or any other) language. For example

entering the religion of Allah (you don't need to translate for فِي because 'enter' means 'go in').	يَدْخُلُوْنَ فِيْ دِيْنِ اللهِ
Forgive me (you don't need to translate for لِ)	اِغْفِرْلِيْ

❸ Sometimes, a preposition may not be there in Arabic but required in English.

I ask forgiveness **of** Allah (you have to add 'of' in English)	أَسْتَغْفِرُ اللهَ
And have mercy **on** me (you have to add 'on' in English)	وَارْحَمْنِيْ

❹ Change of preposition leads to change in the meanings. This is true perhaps for any language. For example, in English, we have: get; get in; get out; get off; get on. Same is true for Arabic. Let us take just two examples.

Pray to your Rabb	صَلِّ لِرَبِّكَ (صَلِّ + لِ)
Send peace on Muhammad (ﷺ)	صَلِّ عَلٰى مُحَمَّد (صَلِّ + عَلَى)

❺ A preposition is followed by a noun and the noun is given by double kasrah on the noun. For example

فِيْ كِتَابٍ، إِلٰى بَيْتٍ

If that noun is specific (i.e., has الْ on it), then we will have a single kasrah on it. For example:

فِي الْكِتَابِ، إِلَى الْبَيْتِ، بِاللهِ، لِلهِ، مِنَ الشَّيْطٰنِ

As you study of the Qur'an progresses, you will be familiar with the use of prepositions, inShaAllah.

Demonstrative Pronouns: Let us learn four words in Arabic that are used to show persons, objects, or actions. These four words occur **953 times** in the Qur'an. Practice them using TPI as described below.

- Point one finger to someone near you and say هٰذَا. Point four fingers in the same direction and say هٰؤُلَآءِ.

- Point one finger towards someone at a distance and say ذٰلِكَ. The direction should not be to the right (for هُوَ، هُمْ) nor to the front (for أَنْتَ، أَنْتُمْ) but in between. Point four fingers in the same direction and say أُولٰئِكَ.

<table>
<tr><td colspan="2" align="center">*** (Spoken Arabic) ***</td><td colspan="2" align="center">(Demonstrative Pronouns)</td></tr>
<tr><td>نَعَمْ، هٰذَا مُسْلِم</td><td>أَهٰذَا مُسْلِم؟</td><td>This</td><td>هٰذَا 225</td></tr>
<tr><td>نَعَمْ، هٰؤُلَآءِ مُسْلِمُونَ</td><td>أَهٰؤُلَآءِ مُسْلِمُونَ؟</td><td>These</td><td>46 هٰؤُلَآءِ</td></tr>
<tr><td>نَعَمْ، ذٰلِكَ مُسْلِم</td><td>أَذٰلِكَ مُسْلِم؟</td><td>That</td><td>478 ذٰلِكَ</td></tr>
<tr><td>نَعَمْ، أُولٰئِكَ مُسْلِمُونَ</td><td>أَأُولٰئِكَ مُسْلِمُونَ؟</td><td>Those</td><td>204 أُولٰئِكَ</td></tr>
</table>

Note: The feminine of هٰذَا is هٰذِهِ [47] and feminine of ذٰلِكَ is تِلْكَ [43] eg:

هٰذِهِ كُرَّاسَةٌ: This is a notebook.

تِلْكَ مَدْرَسَةٌ: That is a school.

After completing this lesson (a & b), you will learn **102 new** words, which occur 27,926 times in the Qur'an.

GRAMMAR: In the previous lessons, we learnt about nouns and letters. Starting with this lesson, we shall concentrate on the verb.

The verb is a word that shows action. For example فَتَحَ (he opened), نَصَرَ (he helped), يَشْرَبُ (he is drinking or he will drink), etc.

Verbs and nouns in Arabic are generally made up of three letters called root letters, for example, فَعَلَ، نَصَرَ، ضَرَبَ, etc. In the Arabic language, there are three tenses; فعل ماضٍ (Perfect tense), فعل مضارع (Imperfect tense), and فعل أمر (Imperative). In this lesson we shall study فعل ماضٍ (Perfect tense), meaning that the work is completed. Let us master the six forms of the فعل ماضٍ through the TPI. You can learn two forms at a time. The methodology is explained below:

- When you say فَعَلَ (He did), point the index finger of the right hand towards your right and imagine a person sitting on your right. Keep the forearm at chest level in a horizontal position. When you say فَعَلُوا (They did), point the four fingers of your right hand in the same direction.
- When you say فَعَلْتَ (You did), point the index finger of your right hand towards your front. When you say فَعَلْتُ (I did), point the index finger of your right hand towards yourself. In a class, the teacher should point his finger towards the students and the students should point their fingers towards the teacher.
- When you say فَعَلْتُمْ (You all did), point the four fingers of your right hand towards your front. When you say فَعَلْنَا (We did) point the four fingers of your right hand towards yourself.

Remember, right-hand directions represent the masculine gender and left hand for feminine gender. Make sure to keep the forearm at a horizontal level for all the directions in فعل ماضٍ.

✿✿✿ Spoken Arabic ✿✿✿

Everyone has done good works; so answer the following using "yes."

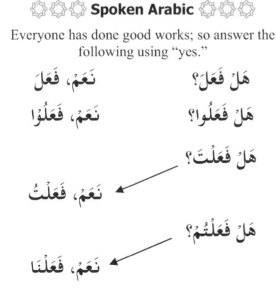

		فعل ماضٍ (ف ع ل) 26	
He did.	فَعَلَ
They all did.	فَعَلُوا
You did.	فَعَلْتَ
I did.	فَعَلْتُ
You all did.	فَعَلْتُمْ
We did.	فَعَلْنَا

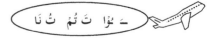

Depending upon the **person**, (3rd, 2nd, 1st) or **number** (singular or plural), the ending words of the past tense change. The change shows who has done the work.

If you are standing in the middle of a road, you can see the backside of a car, a truck or a jeep that is gone. Something that has taken off or has gone, represents the past. A look at the backside is enough for you to tell which type of vehicle has gone. Instead of drawing all these, we show an airplane taking off while you are standing in the middle of the runway. Looking at the ending letters, you can say who has done the work, you, him, or me. These ending words are: (ـ، وا، تَ، تُ، تُمْ، نَا)

Some more points to remember:

- أَنْتَ فَعَلْتَ – أَنْتُمْ فَعَلْتُم : You can notice the relationship clearly between تَ تَ and تُمْ.

- نَحْنُ فَعَلْنَا : Both have the letter ن.

Let us take another verb فَتَحَ: he opened.

فعل ماضٍ (ف ت ح) 8	
He opened.	فَتَحَ
They all opened.	فَتَحُوا
You opened.	فَتَحْتَ
I opened.	فَتَحْتُ
You all opened.	فَتَحْتُمْ
We opened.	فَتَحْنَا

Spoken Arabic: You have opened the books before; so, answer the following using 'yes.'

هَلْ فَتَحَ؟   نَعَمْ، فَتَحَ

هَلْ فَتَحُوا؟   نَعَمْ، فَتَحُوا

هَلْ فَتَحْتَ؟

نَعَمْ، فَتَحْتُ

هَلْ فَتَحْتُمْ؟

نَعَمْ، فَتَحْنَا

The verb جَعَلَ[233] (He made) is similar to فَعَلَ and فَتَحَ. Make sure to practice its past tense forms as homework.

جَعَلْنَا   جَعَلْتُمْ   جَعَلْتُ   جَعَلْتَ   جَعَلُوا   جَعَلَ   233

Lesson 10b

فعل ماضٍ: نَصَرَ، خَلَقَ، ذَكَرَ، عَبَدَ

After completing this lesson (a & b), you will learn **116 new** words, which occur **28,854** times in the Qur'an.

Spoken Arabic

هَلْ نَصَرَ زَيْدًا؟*	نَعَمْ، نَصَرَ زَيْدًا
هَلْ نَصَرُوْا زَيْدًا؟	نَعَمْ، نَصَرُوْا زَيْدًا
هَلْ نَصَرْتَ زَيْدًا؟	نَعَمْ، نَصَرْتُ زَيْدًا
هَلْ نَصَرْتُمْ زَيْدًا؟	نَعَمْ، نَصَرْنَا زَيْدًا

فعل ماضٍ (ن ص ر) 10	
نَصَرَ	He helped
نَصَرُوا	They helped
نَصَرْتَ	You helped
نَصَرْتُ	I helped
نَصَرْتُمْ	You all helped
نَصَرْنَا	We helped

* If زَيْد comes as the subject then it will be زَيْدٌ, and when it comes as object then it will be زَيْدًا.

Did he help Zaid? هَلْ نَصَرَ زَيْدًا؟*

Let us take خَلَقَ, a verb similar to نَصَرَ. After learning the table, practice spoken Arabic sentences keeping in mind that only Allah is the Creator. Also, note that فعل ماضٍ is negated by مَا. Note: 283 شَيْء: thing. Its plural is أَشْيَاء. We have learnt this word in the prayer after Rukoo''.

Spoken Arabic

هَلْ خَلَقَ شَيْـئًا؟*	مَا خَلَقَ شَيْـئًا
هَلْ خَلَقُوْا شَيْـئًا؟	مَا خَلَقُوْا شَيْـئًا
هَلْ خَلَقْتَ شَيْـئًا؟	مَا خَلَقْتُ شَيْـئًا
هَلْ خَلَقْتُمْ شَيْـئًا؟	مَا خَلَقْنَا شَيْـئًا

فعل ماضٍ (خ ل ق) 150	
خَلَقَ	He created
خَلَقُوْا	They created
خَلَقْتَ	You created
خَلَقْتُ	I created
خَلَقْتُمْ	You all created
خَلَقْنَا	We created

* If شَيْء comes as the subject then it will be شَيْءٌ, and when it comes as object then it will be شَيْـئًا.

Did he create anything? هَلْ خَلَقَ شَيْـئًا؟

Just like نَصَرَ and خَلَقَ forms written above, you can make different forms of ذَكَرَ (He remembered) and عَبَدَ (He worshipped). That is your homework!

7	ذَكَرَ	ذَكَرُوْا	ذَكَرْتَ	ذَكَرْتُ	ذَكَرْتُمْ	ذَكَرْنَا
5	عَبَدَ	عَبَدُوْا	عَبَدْتَّ	عَبَدْتُّ	عَبَدْتُّمْ	عَبَدْنَا

Lesson 11b

فعل ماضٍ: ضَرَبَ، سَمِعَ، عَلِمَ، عَمِلَ

After completing this lesson (a & b), you will learn **131 new** words, which occur **30,797** times in the Qur'an.

✿✿✿ Spoken Arabic ✿✿✿

Answer the following questions keeping in mind that you did not hit anybody.

فعل ماضٍ (ف ت ح) 22	
He hit.	ضَرَبَ
They hit.	ضَرَبُوا
You hit.	ضَرَبْتَ
I hit.	ضَرَبْتُ
You all hit.	ضَرَبْتُمْ
We hit.	ضَرَبْنَا

مَا ضَرَبَ زَيْدًا*   هَلْ ضَرَبَ زَيْدًا؟

مَا ضَرَبُوا زَيْدًا   هَلْ ضَرَبُوا زَيْدًا؟

هَلْ ضَرَبْتَ زَيْدًا؟

مَا ضَرَبْتُ زَيْدًا ←

هَلْ ضَرَبْتُمْ زَيْدًا؟

مَا ضَرَبْنَا زَيْدًا ←

To answer in negative for فعل ماضٍ, use مَا. Therefore مَا ضَرَبَ زَيْدًا : He did not hit Zaid.

In other words مَاضٍ is negated with مَا. For example,

مَا ضَرَبَ، مَا ضَرَبُوا ، مَا ضَرَبْتَ ، مَا ضَرَبْتُ، مَا ضَرَبْتُمْ، مَا ضَرَبْنَا۔

✿✿✿ Spoken Arabic ✿✿✿

Answer the following questions keeping in mind that you heard the Qur'an

فعل ماضٍ (س م ع) 30	
He listened.	سَمِعَ
They listened.	سَمِعُوا
You listened.	سَمِعْتَ
I listened.	سَمِعْتُ
You all listened.	سَمِعْتُمْ
We listened.	سَمِعْنَا

نَعَمْ، سَمِعَ الْقُرْاٰنَ   هَلْ سَمِعَ الْقُرْاٰنَ؟*

نَعَمْ، سَمِعُوا الْقُرْاٰنَ   هَلْ سَمِعُوا الْقُرْاٰنَ؟

هَلْ سَمِعْتَ الْقُرْاٰنَ؟

نَعَمْ، سَمِعْتُ الْقُرْاٰنَ ←

هَلْ سَمِعْتُمُ الْقُرْاٰنَ؟

نَعَمْ، سَمِعْنَا الْقُرْاٰنَ ←

* If الْقُرْاٰن comes as a subject, it will be الْقُرْاٰنُ, and when it comes as object, it will be الْقُرْاٰنَ.

Did he listen to the Qur'an?   هَلْ سَمِعَ الْقُرْاٰنَ؟

Just like سَمِعَ forms written above, you can make different forms of عَلِمَ (He Knew) and عَمِلَ (He did). That is your homework!

| عَلِمْنَا | عَلِمْتُمْ | عَلِمْتُ | عَلِمْتَ | عَلِمُوا | عَلِمَ | 35 |
| عَمِلْنَا | عَمِلْتُمْ | عَمِلْتُ | عَمِلْتَ | عَمِلُوا | عَمِلَ | 99 |

Lesson 12b

فعل مضارع: يَفْعَلُ، يَجْعَلُ، يَفْتَحُ

After completing this lesson (a & b), you will learn **144 new** words, which occur **31,638** times in the Qur'an.

GRAMMAR: In the last three lessons, we learnt فعل ماضٍ (Perfect Tense) representing the action which has been done. Now let us learn فعل مضارع (Imperfect tense). It includes present as well as future tense. It represents the action which is not done yet; it is being done or will be done.

Approximately 8500 words **of the Qur'an are in an Imperfect tense, i.e., almost one in every line of the Qur'an! Learn them thoroughly.**

Practice the فعل مضارع forms using TPI just like you practiced the فعل ماضٍ except the following:

❶ Keep your hand at eye level as opposed to chest level. In فعل ماضٍ, the work was completed and therefore the hand level is down. In فعل مضارع, the work will start or is going on and therefore the hand level is high.

❷ Practice in a louder pitch for فعل مضارع as opposed to a lower pitch for فعل ماضٍ. What is done is past, gone. So, the voice is low for فعل ماضٍ.

❸ Make sure to learn two forms at a time to make it easy. After learning the six terms, you can then repeat the whole table of فعل مضارع.

❀❀❀ **Spoken Arabic** ❀❀❀

نَعَمْ، يَفْعَلُ   هَلْ يَفْعَلُ؟

نَعَمْ، يَفْعَلُوْنَ   هَلْ يَفْعَلُوْنَ؟

هَلْ تَفْعَلُ؟

نَعَمْ، أَفْعَلُ

هَلْ تَفْعَلُوْنَ؟

نَعَمْ، نَفْعَلُ

فعل ماضٍ	فعل مضارع (ف ع ل) 54	
فَعَلَ	يَفْعَلُ	He does / will do.
فَعَلُوْا	يَفْعَلُوْنَ	They do / will do.
فَعَلْتَ	تَفْعَلُ	You do / will do.
فَعَلْتُ	أَفْعَلُ	I do / will do.
فَعَلْتُمْ	تَفْعَلُوْنَ	You all do / will do
فَعَلْنَا	نَفْعَلُ	We do / will do.

ي تَ أ

In case of فعل ماضٍ forms, the endings were changing. For فعل مضارع forms, the change occurs at the start. To remember this, use the following tip.

If you are standing in the middle of a road, you can see only the front end of a car, truck or jeep that is coming towards you. Something that is coming represents فعل مضارع. A look at the front end is enough for you to tell which type of vehicle is coming. Instead of drawing different vehicles, we show a landing airplane while you are standing in the middle of the runway. Looking at the starting letters, you can say who is doing or will do the work, you, him, or me. These starting letters are: (يَ تَ أ نَ).

Another tip to remember the imperfect tense:

- Imagine your friend Yasir sitting on your right planting a small plant. Yasir appears very big next to the small sapling and therefore you see him first. Remember the يْ of يَاسِر. This يْ corresponds to the first letter of يَفْعَلُ. When too many 'Yasirs' work, we would hear the sounds ون, corresponding to the ending in يَفْعَلُوْنَ!

- Likewise, imagine Mr. Tawfeeq in front of you, planting a sapling. Tawfeeq would appear very big in front of the small plant and therefore you see him first. The تَ of تَوفِيق corresponds to the تَ of تَفْعَلُ. When too many 'Tawfeeqs' work, we would again hear the sounds ون, corresponding to the ending in تَفْعَلُوْنَ!

- We have أَنَا for I. The أ from أَنَا corresponds to the أ of أَفْعَلُ.

- The نَ of نَحْنُ corresponds to the نَ of نَفْعَلُ. Remember that the word is نَفْعَلُ and not نَفْعَلُوْنَ. When we (نَحْنُ) work, we should do it quietly! Do not make any sounds (ون)!

- In short, in the perfect tense, the endings change (ـَ وا تَ تُمْ ثُ نَا) whereas, in the imperfect tense, it is the beginnings that change (يَ تَ أ نَ).

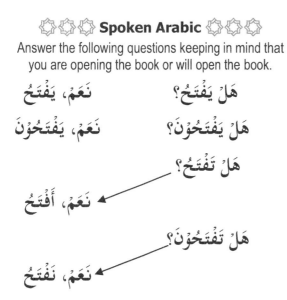

✵✵✵ **Spoken Arabic** ✵✵✵
Answer the following questions keeping in mind that you are opening the book or will open the book.

هَلْ يَفْتَحُ؟   نَعَمْ، يَفْتَحُ

هَلْ يَفْتَحُوْنَ؟   نَعَمْ، يَفْتَحُوْنَ

هَلْ تَفْتَحُ؟

نَعَمْ، أَفْتَحُ

هَلْ تَفْتَحُوْنَ؟

نَعَمْ، نَفْتَحُ

فعل ماضٍ	فعل مضارع (ف ت ح) 2	
فَتَحَ	يَفْتَحُ	He opens/ will open
فَتَحُوا	يَفْتَحُوْنَ	They open/ will open
فَتَحْتَ	تَفْتَحُ	You open/ will open
فَتَحْتُ	أَفْتَحُ	I open/ will open
فَتَحْتُمْ	تَفْتَحُوْنَ	You all open/ will open
فَتَحْنَا	نَفْتَحُ	We open/ will open

Just like فَتَحَ يَفْتَحُ forms written above, you can make different forms of جَعَلَ يَجْعَلُ (He makes/ will make). That is your homework!

نَجْعَلُ   تَجْعَلُوْنَ   أَجْعَلُ   تَجْعَلُ   يَجْعَلُوْنَ   يَجْعَلُ   83

فعل مضارع: يَنْصُرُ، يَخْلُقُ، يَذْكُرُ، يَعْبُدُ

> After completing this lesson (a & b), you will learn **156 new** words, which occur **32,111** times in the Qur'an.

✿✿✿ **Spoken Arabic** ✿✿✿

فعل مضارع (ن ص ر) 28		فعل ماضٍ
He helps/ will help	يَنْصُرُ	نَصَرَ
They help/ will help	يَنْصُرُوْنَ	نَصَرُوْا
You help/ will help	تَنْصُرُ	نَصَرْتَ
I help/ will help	أَنْصُرُ	نَصَرْتُ
You all help/ will help	تَنْصُرُوْنَ	نَصَرْتُمْ
We help/ will help	نَنْصُرُ	نَصَرْنَا

نَعَمْ، يَنْصُرُ زَيْدًا   هَلْ يَنْصُرُ زَيْدًا؟*

نَعَمْ، يَنْصُرونَ زَيْدًا   هَلْ يَنْصُرُوْنَ زَيْدًا؟

هَلْ تَنْصُرُ زَيْدًا؟

نَعَمْ، أَنْصُرُ زَيْدًا

هَلْ تَنْصُرُوْنَ زَيْدًا؟

نَعَمْ، نَنْصُرُ زَيْدًا

* If زَيْدٌ comes as the subject then it will be زَيْدٌ, and when it comes as object then it will be زَيْدًا.

هَلْ يَنْصُرُ زَيْدًا؟*   Does he help Zaid?

✿✿✿ **Spoken Arabic** ✿✿✿

فعل مضارع (خ ل ق) 23		فعل ماضٍ
He creates/ will create	يَخْلُقُ	خَلَقَ
They create/ will create	يَخْلُقُوْنَ	خَلَقُوْا
You create/ will create	تَخْلُقُ	خَلَقْتَ
I create/ will create	أَخْلُقُ	خَلَقْتُ
You all create/ will create	تَخْلُقُوْنَ	خَلَقْتُمْ
We create/ will create	نَخْلُقُ	خَلَقْنَا

لَا يَخْلُقُ شَيْئًا   هَلْ يَخْلُقُ شَيْئًا؟*

لَا يَخْلُقُوْنَ شَيْئًا   هَلْ يَخْلُقُوْنَ شَيْئًا؟

هَلْ تَخْلُقُ شَيْئًا؟

لَا أَخْلُقُ شَيْئًا

هَلْ تَخْلُقُوْنَ شَيْئًا؟

لَا نَخْلُقُ شَيْئًا

When you want to negate, you may use لَا or مَا, as shown below:

لَا يَخْلُقُ، لَا يَخْلُقُوْنَ، لَا تَخْلُقُ، لَا أَخْلُقُ، لَا تَخْلُقُوْنَ، لَا نَخْلُقُ | مَا يَخْلُقُ، مَا يَخْلُقُوْنَ، مَا تَخْلُقُ، مَا أَخْلُقُ، مَا تَخْلُقُوْنَ، مَا نَخْلُقُ

* If شَيْء comes as the subject then it will be شَيْءٌ, and when it comes as object then it will be شَيْئًا.

هَلْ يَخْلُقُ شَيْئًا؟   Does he create anything?

Just like نَصَرَ يَنْصُرُ forms written above, you can make different forms of ذَكَرَ يَذْكُرُ (He remembers/ will remember) and عَبَدَ يَعْبُدُ (He worships/ will worship). That is your homework!

نَذْكُرُ	تَذْكُرُوْنَ	أَذْكُرُ	تَذْكُرُ	يَذْكُرُوْنَ	يَذْكُرُ	17
نَعْبُدُ	تَعْبُدُوْنَ	أَعْبُدُ	تَعْبُدُ	يَعْبُدُوْنَ	يَعْبُدُ	80

Lesson 14b

فعل مضارع: يَضْرِبُ، يَسْمَعُ، يَعْلَمُ، يَعْمَلُ

After completing this lesson (a & b), you will learn **174 new** words, which occur **36,556** times in the Qur'an.

You have learnt نَصَرَ، يَنْصُرُ and فَتَحَ، يَفْتَحُ. Now, let us take the third style: ضَرَبَ، يَضْرِبُ.

فعل ماضٍ	فعل مضارع (ف ع ل) 13	
ضَرَبَ	يَضْرِبُ	He hits/ will hit.
ضَرَبُوا	يَضْرِبُوْنَ	They hit/ will hit.
ضَرَبْتَ	تَضْرِبُ	You hit/ will hit.
ضَرَبْتُ	أَضْرِبُ	I hit/ will hit.
ضَرَبْتُمْ	تَضْرِبُوْنَ	You all hit/ will hit.
ضَرَبْنَا	نَضْرِبُ	We hit/ will hit.

The last style is: سَمِعَ، يَسْمَعُ. Let us learn all the forms for this verb.

❁❁❁ **Spoken Arabic** ❁❁❁

فعل ماضٍ	فعل مضارع (س م ع) 39	
سَمِعَ	يَسْمَعُ	He listens/ will listen.
سَمِعُوا	يَسْمَعُوْنَ	They listen/ will listen.
سَمِعْتَ	تَسْمَعُ	You listen/ will listen.
سَمِعْتُ	أَسْمَعُ	I listen/ will listen.
سَمِعْتُمْ	تَسْمَعُوْنَ	You all listen/ will listen.
سَمِعْنَا	نَسْمَعُ	We listen/ will listen.

مَاذَا يَسْمَعُ؟*   يَسْمَعُ الْقُرْاٰنَ

مَاذَا يَسْمَعُوْنَ؟   يَسْمَعُوْنَ الْقُرْاٰنَ

مَاذَا تَسْمَعُ؟

أَسْمَعُ الْقُرْاٰنَ

مَاذَا تَسْمَعُوْنَ؟

نَسْمَعُ الْقُرْاٰنَ

* If you want to ask regarding the action, you should use مَاذَا (what).

مَاذَا يَسْمَعُ؟   What does he listen to?

Just like سَمِعَ يَسْمَعُ forms written above, you can make different forms of عَلِمَ يَعْلَمُ (He knows/ will know). and عَمِلَ يَعْمَلُ (He does/ will do). That is your homework!

| نَعْلَمُ | تَعْلَمُوْنَ | أَعْلَمُ | تَعْلَمُ | يَعْلَمُوْنَ | يَعْلَمُ | 362 |
| نَعْمَلُ | تَعْمَلُوْنَ | أَعْمَلُ | تَعْمَلُ | يَعْمَلُوْنَ | يَعْمَلُ | 166 |

Lesson 15b

فعل أمر ونهي: اِفْعَلْ، اِفْتَحْ، اِجْعَلْ

After completing this lesson (a & b), you will learn **186 new** words, which occur **37,500** times in the Qur'an.

GRAMMAR: In this lesson, we will learn to make **imperative** and **prohibitive** forms of a verb.

- When you say اِفْعَلْ, point the index finger of your right hand toward the one in front of you and move your hand down from a raised position as if you are giving a command to somebody in front of you. When you say اِفْعَلُوْا, repeat the same with four fingers.

- When you say لَا تَفْعَلْ, point the index finger of your right hand and move the hand from left to right as if you are asking somebody not to do something. When you say لَا تَفْعَلُوْا, repeat the same with four fingers.

- سَوْفَ: Soon;   سَ: Very soon;   لَنْ: never

✧✧ Spoken Arabic ✧✧

سَوْفَ أَفْعَلُ	اِفْعَلْ!
سَوْفَ نَفْعَلُ	اِفْعَلُوْا

فعل أمر، فعل نهي، (3) اسم فاعل، اسم مفعول، Name of action		فعل مضارع	فعل ماضٍ
Do!	اِفْعَلْ	يَفْعَلُ	فَعَلَ
Do! (you all)	اِفْعَلُوْا	يَفْعَلُوْنَ	فَعَلُوْا
Don't do!	لَا تَفْعَلْ	تَفْعَلُ	فَعَلْتَ
Don't do!	لَا تَفْعَلُوْا	أَفْعَلُ	فَعَلْتُ
		تَفْعَلُوْنَ	فَعَلْتُمْ
		نَفْعَلُ	فَعَلْنَا

✧✧ Spoken Arabic ✧✧

سَوْفَ أَفْتَحُ	اِفْتَحْ!
سَوْفَ نَفْتَحُ	اِفْتَحُوْا!

فعل أمر، فعل نهي، (2) اسم فاعل، اسم مفعول، Name of action		فعل مضارع	فعل ماضٍ
Open!	اِفْتَحْ	يَفْتَحُ	فَتَحَ
Open! (you all)	اِفْتَحُوْا	يَفْتَحُوْنَ	فَتَحُوْا
Don't open!	لَا تَفْتَحْ	تَفْتَحُ	فَتَحْتَ
Don't open!	لَا تَفْتَحُوْا	أَفْتَحُ	فَتَحْتُ
		تَفْتَحُوْنَ	فَتَحْتُمْ
		نَفْتَحُ	فَتَحْنَا

Just like فَتَحَ forms written above, you can make different forms of جَعَلَ. That is your homework!

Don't make!	لَا تَجْعَلُوْا	Don't make!	لَا تَجْعَلْ	Make! (you all)	اِجْعَلُوْا	Make!	اِجْعَلْ

22

فعل أمر ونهى: أُنْصُرْ، أُذْكُرْ، أُعْبُدْ، أُخْلُقْ

After completing this lesson (a & b), you will learn **194 new** words, which occur **38,531** times in the Qur'an.

Let us learn the أمر and نهي forms of the four verbs: نَصَرَ، ذَكَرَ، عَبَدَ، خَلَقَ .

✦✦ Spoken Arabic ✦✦

٤٢ سَوْفَ أَنْصُرُ زَيْدًا!   أُنْصُرْ زَيْدًا!

سَوْفَ نَنْصُرُ زَيْدًا!   أُنْصُرُوا زَيْدًا!

فعل أمر، فعل نَهى، (7) اسم فاعل، اسم مفعول، Name of action		فعل مضارع	فعل ماضٍ
Help!	أُنْصُرْ	يَنْصُرُ	نَصَرَ
Help! (You all)	أُنْصُرُوا	يَنْصُرُونَ	نَصَرُوا
Don't help!	لَا تَنْصُرْ	تَنْصُرُ	نَصَرَتْ
Don't help!	لَا تَنْصُرُوا	أَنْصُرُ	نَصَرْتُ
		تَنْصُرُونَ	نَصَرْتُمْ
		نَنْصُرُ	نَصَرْنَا

✦✦ Spoken Arabic ✦✦

سَوْفَ أَذْكُرُ الرَّحْمٰنَ!   أُذْكُرِ الرَّحْمٰنَ!

سَوْفَ نَذْكُرُ الرَّحْمٰنَ!   أُذْكُرُوا الرَّحْمٰنَ!

فعل أمر فعل نَهى، (48) اسم فاعل، اسم مفعول، Name of action		فعل مضارع	فعل ماضٍ
Remember!	أُذْكُرْ	يَذْكُرُ	ذَكَرَ
Remember! (you all)	أُذْكُرُوا	يَذْكُرُونَ	ذَكَرُوا
Don't Remember!	لَا تَذْكُرْ	تَذْكُرُ	ذَكَرَتْ
Don't Remember!	لَا تَذْكُرُوا	أَذْكُرُ	ذَكَرْتُ
		تَذْكُرُونَ	ذَكَرْتُمْ
		نَذْكُرُ	ذَكَرْنَا

Just like نَصَرَ and خَلَقَ forms written above, you can make different forms of عَبَدَ and خَلَقَ. That is your homework!

Don't Worship! You all	لَا تَعْبُدُوا	Don't Worship!	لَا تَعْبُدْ	Worship! You all	أُعْبُدُوا	Worship!	أُعْبُدْ	37
Don't Create! You all	لَا تَخْلُقُوا	Don't Create!	لَا تَخْلُقْ	Create! You all	أُخْلُقُوا	Create!	أُخْلُقْ	

Lesson
17b

فعل أمر ونهى: اِضْرِب، اِسْمَعْ، اِعْلَمْ، اِعْمَلْ

After completing this lesson (a & b),
you will learn **208 new** words, which
occur **39,571** times in the Qur'an.

Let us learn the أمر and نهي forms of the verb: ضَرَبَ يَضْرِبُ.

🌸 Spoken Arabic 🌸

فعل أمر، فعل نهى، (12) Name of action، اسم فاعل، اسم مفعول		فعل مضارع	فعل ماضٍ
Hit!	اِضْرِب	يَضْرِبُ	ضَرَبَ
Hit! (You all)	اِضْرِبُوا	يَضْرِبُونَ	ضَرَبُوا
Don't hit!	لَا تَضْرِب	تَضْرِبُ	ضَرَبْتَ
Don't hit! (You all)	لَا تَضْرِبُوا	أَضْرِبُ	ضَرَبْتُ
		تَضْرِبُونَ	ضَرَبْتُمْ
		نَضْرِبُ	ضَرَبْنَا

سَوْفَ أَضْرِبُ الْكُرَةَ ‏‏‏‏‏‏‏‏‏‏ اِضْرِبِ الْكُرَةَ!
سَوْفَ نَضْرِبُ الْكُرَةَ ‏‏‏‏‏‏‏‏‏‏ اِضْرِبُوا الْكُرَةَ!

Let us learn the أمر and نهي forms of the verb سَمِعَ يَسْمَعُ.

🌸 Spoken Arabic 🌸

فعل أمر، فعل نهى، (7) Name of action، اسم فاعل، اسم مفعول		فعل مضارع	فعل ماضٍ
Listen!	اِسْمَعْ	يَسْمَعُ	سَمِعَ
Listen! (You all)	اِسْمَعُوا	يَسْمَعُونَ	سَمِعُوا
Don't Listen!	لَا تَسْمَعْ	تَسْمَعُ	سَمِعْتَ
Don't Listen! (You all)	لَا تَسْمَعُوا	أَسْمَعُ	سَمِعْتُ
		تَسْمَعُونَ	سَمِعْتُمْ
		نَسْمَعُ	سَمِعْنَا

سَوْفَ أَسْمَعُ الْقُرْاٰنَ ‏‏‏‏‏‏‏‏ اِسْمَعِ الْقُرْاٰنَ!
سَوْفَ نَسْمَعُ الْقُرْاٰنَ ‏‏‏‏‏‏‏‏ اِسْمَعُوا الْقُرْاٰنَ!

Just like سَمِعَ forms written above, you can make different forms of عَلِمَ and عَمِلَ. That is your homework!

Don't know! (You all)	لَا تَعْلَمُوا	Don't Know!	لَا تَعْلَمْ	Know! (You all)	اِعْلَمُوا	Know!	اِعْلَمْ	31

Don't Do (You all)	لَا تَعْمَلُوا	Don't Do!	لَا تَعْمَلْ	Do! (you all)	اِعْمَلُوا	Do!	اِعْمَلْ	11

Lesson 18b

اسم فاعل، اسم مفعول، :Name of action

فَعَلَ، فَتَحَ، جَعَلَ...

After completing this lesson (a & b), you will learn **222 new** words, which occur **40,469** times in the Qur'an.

GRAMMAR: Let us learn to make the 3 forms: فَاعِل، مفعُول، فِعل

There was a time when Muslims used to give knowledge, art, technology, to the world. Now the opposite is happening because we left the Qur'an. Remember "to give."

When you say فَاعِل (doer), show it with your right hand as if you are giving, i.e., doing something good. Giving a coin to someone in charity!

When you say مَفعُول (the one who is affected), show it with your right hand as if you are receiving something. Receive a coin in your palm!

While saying فِعل (to do), move your right hand by making a fist raised high as if you are showing the power of the action.

The plural of فَاعِل is فَاعِلُون or فَاعِلِين.

The plural of مَفعُول is مَفعُولُون or مَفعُولِين.

The number written next to the فَاعِل indicates the occurrence of the words فَاعِل، مَفعُول، فِعل (i.e., the 3 forms) in the Qur'an.

✦✦✦ **Spoken Arabic** ✦✦✦

All of us are doing some good work, الحمد لله

فعل أمر، فعل نهى، اسم فاعل، اسم مفعول Name of action		فعل مضارع	فعل ماضٍ
Do!	اِفْعَلْ	يَفْعَلُ	فَعَلَ
Do! (you all)	اِفْعَلُوا	يَفْعَلُونَ	فَعَلُوا
Don't do!	لَا تَفْعَلْ	تَفْعَلُ	فَعَلَتْ
Don't do!	لَا تَفْعَلُوا	أَفْعَلُ	فَعَلْتُ
Doer the one who is affected to do	**17** فَاعِل مَفْعُول فِعْل	تَفْعَلُونَ نَفْعَلُ	فَعَلْتُمْ فَعَلْنَا

نَعَمْ، أَنَا فَاعِلٌ   هَلْ أَنْتَ فَاعِلٌ؟

نَعَمْ، نَحْنُ فَاعِلُونَ   هَلْ أَنْتُمْ فَاعِلُونَ؟

✦✦✦ **Spoken Arabic** ✦✦✦

You must have opened a door.

فعل أمر، فعل نهى، اسم فاعل، اسم مفعول Name of action		فعل مضارع	فعل ماضٍ
Open!	اِفْتَحْ	يَفْتَحُ	فَتَحَ
Open! (you all)	اِفْتَحُوا	يَفْتَحُونَ	فَتَحُوا
Don't open!	لَا تَفْتَحْ	تَفْتَحُ	فَتَحَتْ
Don't open!	لَا تَفْتَحُوا	أَفْتَحُ	فَتَحْتُ
Opener The one which is opened To open	**13** فَاتِح مَفْتُوح فَتْح	تَفْتَحُونَ نَفْتَحُ	فَتَحْتُمْ فَتَحْنَا

نَعَمْ، أَنَا فَاتِح   هَلْ أَنْتَ فَاتِح؟

نَعَمْ،الْمَسْجِدُ مَفْتُوح   هَلِ الْمَسْجِدُ مَفْتُوح؟

۞۞۞ Spoken Arabic ۞۞۞

You might have made something good!
Therefore, answer in yes!

فعل أمر، فعل نهى، اسم فاعل، اسم مفعول، Name of action		فعل مضارع	فعل ماضٍ
Make!	إِجْعَلْ	يَجْعَلُ	جَعَلَ
Make! (you all)	إِجْعَلُوا	يَجْعَلُونَ	جَعَلُوا
Don't make!	لَا تَجْعَلْ	تَجْعَلُ	جَعَلَتْ
Don't make!	لَا تَجْعَلُوا	أَجْعَلُ	جَعَلْتُ
Maker	جَاعِل 6	تَجْعَلُونَ	جَعَلْتُمْ
That which is made	مَجْعُول	نَجْعَلُ	جَعَلْنَا
To make	جَعْل		

هَلْ أَنْتَ جَاعِل؟   نَعَمْ، أَنَا جَاعِل

هَلْ أَنْتُمْ جَاعِلُوْنَ؟   نَعَمْ، نَحْنُ جَاعِلُوْن

۞۞۞ Spoken Arabic ۞۞۞

The real helper is Allah. He is نَاصِر. All of us are
helped by Allah. We are مَنْصُوْرُوْن.

فعل أمر، فعل نهى، اسم فاعل، اسم مفعول، Name of action		فعل مضارع	فعل ماضٍ
Help!	أُنْصُرْ	يَنْصُرُ	نَصَرَ
Help! (You all)	أُنْصُرُوا	يَنْصُرُونَ	نَصَرُوا
Don't help!	لَا تَنْصُرْ	تَنْصُرُ	نَصَرَتْ
Don't help!	لَا تَنْصُرُوا	أَنْصُرُ	نَصَرْتُ
Helper	نَاصِر 35	تَنْصُرُونَ	نَصَرْتُمْ
The one who is helped	مَنْصُوْر	نَنْصُرُ	نَصَرْنَا
Help, to help	نَصْر		

هَلْ هُوَ نَاصِر؟   نَعَمْ، هُوَ نَاصِر

هَلْ أَنْتَ مَنْصُوْر؟   نَعَمْ، أَنَا مَنْصُوْر

Following the same style, you can make the forms for ذَكَرَ and خَلَق. That is your homework!

Creation, to create	خَلْق	The one who is created	مَخْلُوْق	Creator	خَالِق
To remember, remembrance	ذِكْر	The one who is remembered	مَذْكُوْر	One who remembers	ذَاكِر	79

Lesson 19b — Name of action اسم فاعل، اسم مفعول

عَبَدَ، ضَرَب، سَمِعَ...

After completing this lesson (a & b), you will learn **232 new** words, which occur **41,111** times in the Qur'an.

✸✸✸ **Spoken Arabic** ✸✸✸

We are the worshippers of Allah.

فعل أمر فعل نهى، اسم فاعل، اسم مفعول، Name of action		فعل مضارع	فعل ماضٍ
Worship!	أُعْبُدْ	يَعْبُدُ	عَبَدَ
Worship! You all	أُعْبُدُوا	يَعْبُدُوْنَ	عَبَدُوْا
Don't Worship!	لَا تَعْبُدْ	تَعْبُدُ	عَبَدَتْ
Don't Worship! You all	لَا تَعْبُدوا	أَعْبُدُ	عَبَدْتُّ
One who worships The one who is worshipped Worship, to worship	20 عَابِد مَعْبُود عِبَادَة	تَعْبُدُوْنَ	عَبَدْتُّمْ
		نَعْبُدُ	عَبَدْنَا

هَلْ أَنْتَ عَابِد؟   نَعَمْ أَنَا عَابِد

هَلْ أَنْتُمْ عَابِدُوْنَ؟   نَعَمْ نَحْنُ عَابِدُوْن

✸✸✸ **Spoken Arabic** ✸✸✸

فعل أمر فعل نهى، اسم فاعل، اسم مفعول، Name of action		فعل مضارع	فعل ماضٍ
Hit!	اِضْرِبْ	يَضْرِبُ	ضَرَبَ
Hit! (You all)	اِضْرِبُوْا	يَضْرِبُوْنَ	ضَرَبُوْا
Don't hit!	لَا تَضْرِب	تَضْرِبُ	ضَرَبْتَ
Don't hit! (You all)	لَا تَضْرِبُوْا	أَضْرِبُ	ضَرَبْتُ
one who hits the one who is hit to hit, hit	3 ضَارِب مَضْرُوْب ضَرْب	تَضْرِبُوْنَ	ضَرَبْتُمْ
		نَضْرِبُ	ضَرَبْنَا

✸✸✸ **Spoken Arabic** ✸✸✸

Are you all listening? Hope your mind is not somewhere else.

فعل أمر فعل نهى، اسم فاعل، اسم مفعول، Name of action		فعل مضارع	فعل ماضٍ
Listen!	اِسْمَعْ	يَسْمَعُ	سَمِعَ
Listen! (You all)	اِسْمَعُوْا	يَسْمَعُوْنَ	سَمِعُوْا
Don't Listen!	لَا تَسْمَعْ	تَسْمَعُ	سَمِعْتَ
Don't Listen (You all)	لَا تَسْمَعُوْا	أَسْمَعُ	سَمِعْتُ
One who listens The one who is listened to To listen	22 سَامِع مَسْمُوْع سَمْع	تَسْمَعُوْنَ	سَمِعْتُمْ
		نَسْمَعُ	سَمِعْنَا

هَلْ أَنْتَ سَامِع؟   نَعَمْ، أَنَا سَامِع

هَلْ أَنْتُمْ سَامِعُوْن؟   نَعَمْ، نَحْنُ سَامِعُوْن

Just like سَمِعَ forms written above, you can make different forms of عَلِمَ and عَمِلَ. That is your homework!

| 134 | عَالِم | The one who knows, scholar | مَعْلُوم | that which is known To know | عِلْم | To know, knowledge |
| 42 | عَامِل | the worker, labour | مَعْمُول | the one is worked upon | عَمَل | To act, to do, work |

Feminine forms

Since the feminine gender is rarely used in the Qur'an, we will learn only one form (3rd person) for the feminine gender using TPI. We use the right hand for masculine gender and left hand for feminine gender for TPI.

| (she does) | هُوَ يَفْعَلُ – هِيَ تَفْعَلُ | (she did) | هُوَ فَعَلَ – هِيَ فَعَلَتْ |

Let us take some more verbs.

(she opens)	هُوَ يَفْتَحُ– هِيَ تَفْتَحُ	(she opened)	هُوَ فَتَحَ – هِيَ فَتَحَتْ
(she helps)	هُوَ يَنْصُرُ – هِيَ تَنْصُرُ	(she helped)	هُوَ نَصَرَ – هِيَ نَصَرَتْ
(she hits)	هُوَ يَضْرِبُ – هِيَ تَضْرِبُ	(she hit)	هُوَ ضَرَبَ – هِيَ ضَرَبَتْ
(she hears)	هُوَ يَسْمَعُ – هِيَ تَسْمَعُ	(she heard)	هُوَ سَمِعَ – هِيَ سَمِعَتْ

Sarf-e-Sagheer (صرف صغير)

After completing this lesson (a & b),
you will learn **232 new** words, which
occur 41,111 times in the Qur'an.

The short formula for remembering the verb forms (Short conjugation):

You have learnt 7 forms for فعل ماضٍ and 7 forms for فعل مضارع and four for أمر ونهي. If we pick up

- فَعَلَ: the key for all فعل ماضٍ forms;
- يَفْعَلُ: the key for all فعل مضارع forms;
- اِفْعَلْ: the key for all فعل أمر forms;

and add the three nouns فاعل، مفْعُول، فِعْل to it, we get the short table for all the basic forms that are made from فَعَلَ.

اسم(اَلْ ئِـئَـ)	اسم(اَلْ ئِـئَـ)	اسم(اَلْ ئِـئَـ)	فعل أمر key	فعل مضارع key	فعل ماضٍ key
فِعْل to do, action	مَفْعُوْل the one who is affected	فَاعِل Doer	اِفْعَلْ Do!	يَفْعَلُ He does will do	فَعَلَ He did
فَتْح To open	مَفْتُوْح The one which is opened	فَاتِح Opener	اِفْتَحْ Open!	يَفْتَحُ He opens will open	فَتَحَ He opened
نَصْر Help, to help	مَنْصُوْر The one who is helped	نَاصِر Helper	اُنْصُرْ Help!	يَنْصُرُ He helps will help	نَصَرَ He helped
ضَرْب to hit, hit	مَضْرُوْب the one who is hit	ضَارِب one who hits	اِضْرِبْ Hit!	يَضْرِبُ He hits. will hit.	ضَرَبَ He hit.
سَمْع To listen	مَسْمُوْع The one who is listened to	سَامِع One who listens	اِسْمَعْ Listen!	يَسْمَعُ He listens. will listen	سَمِعَ He listened

In Arabic, objects such as "him," "them," etc. are attached to the verbs very frequently. We are taking a verb نَصَرَ to show how it is used in the Qur'an.

فعل ماضٍ

نَعَمْ نَصَرْتُ زَيْدًا۔	هَلْ نَصَرْتَ زَيْدًا؟
نَعَمْ نَصَرْنَا زَيْدًا۔	هَلْ نَصَرْتُمْ زَيْدًا؟

Now use " هُ " instead of زَيْدًا. Even though " هُ " is attached to the verb, give a pause while practising the following sentences before it.

نَعَمْ نَصَرْتُهُ (نَصَرْتُ ـهُ)	هَلْ نَصَرْتَهُ؟ (نَصَرْتَ ـهُ)
نَعَمْ نَصَرْنَاهُ (نَصَرْنَا هُ)	هَلْ نَصَرْتُمُوهُ؟ (نَصَرْتُمُو هُ)

<u>Note</u>: نَصَرْتُمُوهُ is recited instead of نَصَرْتُمُهُ for ease of pronunciation.

فعل مضارع

نَعَمْ أَنْصُرُ زَيْدًا۔	هَلْ تَنْصُرُ زَيْدًا؟
نَعَمْ نَنْصُرُ زَيْدًا۔	هَلْ تَنْصُرُونَ زَيْدًا؟

Now use " هُ " instead of زَيْدًا. Even though " هُ " is attached to the verb, give a pause while practising the following sentences before it.

نَعَمْ أَنْصُرُهُ (أَنْصُرُ ـهُ)	هَلْ تَنْصُرُهُ؟ (تَنْصُرُ ـهُ)
نَعَمْ نَنْصُرُهُ (نَنْصُرُ هُ)	هَلْ تَنْصُرُونَهُ؟ (تَنْصُرُونَ هُ)

Workbook

Q1: Translate the following.

الرَّجِيْمِ	مِنَ الشَّيْطٰنِ	بِاللهِ	اَعُوْذُ

Q2: Fill up the table below?

No. of pages in Mushaf	
No. of lines in each page	
No. of words in each line	
No. of words in a page	
Total Words in the Qur'an	
Words of this course in the Qur'an	

Q3: What are the 6 objectives of this course?
Ans:

Q4: What are the benefits of starting to learn Arabic through Salah?
Ans:

Q5: How can we improve our focus in Salah.
Ans:

Lesson 2a   Surah Al-Fatihah (1-3)

Q1: Translate the following.

الرَّحِيْمِ ①	الرَّحْمٰنِ	اللهِ	بِسْمِ

الرَّحِيْمِ ③ الرَّحْمٰنِ	الْعٰلَمِيْنَ ②	رَبِّ	لِلّٰهِ	اَلْحَمْدُ

Q2: What habits can we learn from "بِسْمِ اللهِ الرَّحْمٰنِ الرَّحِيْمِ"?

Ans:

Q3: Explain the difference between the meanings of اَلرَّحْمٰنِ and اَلرَّحِيْمِ?

Ans:

Q4: What should we do when we get any blessing or reward?

Ans:

Q5: Allah shows mercy to whom in the world and to whom in the Hereafter?

Ans:

Q1: Translate the following.

مٰلِكِ	يَوْمِ	الدِّيْنِ ۴

اِيَّاكَ	نَعْبُدُ	وَاِيَّاكَ	نَسْتَعِيْنُ ۵

Q2: How should we prepare for the Day of Judgment?

Ans:

Q3: Describe different types of عِبَادَة (worship)?

Ans:

Q4: What is the purpose of our lives?

Ans:

Q5: For what do we seek Allah's help?

Ans:

Q1: Translate the following.

اِهْدِنَا	الصِّرَاطَ	الْمُسْتَقِيمَ ٦

صِرَاطَ	الَّذِينَ	اَنْعَمْتَ	عَلَيْهِمْ

غَيْرِ	الْمَغْضُوبِ	عَلَيْهِمْ	وَلَا	الضَّآلِّينَ ٧

Q2: From where can we get Hidayah?
Ans:

Q3: Which categories of people are favored by Allah?
Ans:

Q4: Who are meant by: "الضَّآلِّينَ" and "الْمَغْضُوبِ عَلَيْهِمْ"?
Ans:

Q5: What is the path of those who were favored by Allah? What is it that they do?
Ans:

Q1: Translate the following.

اَللّٰهُ أَكْبَرُ اَللّٰهُ أَكْبَرُ	اَللّٰهُ أَكْبَرُ اَللّٰهُ أَكْبَرُ

اَللّٰهُ	إِلَّا	إِلٰهَ	لَا	أَنْ	أَشْهَدُ

رَّسُوْلُ اللهِ	مُحَمَّدًا	أَنَّ	أَشْهَدُ

الْفَلَاحِ	حَيَّ عَلَى	الصَّلٰوةِ	حَيَّ عَلَى

لَا إِلٰهَ إِلَّا اللهُ.	اَللّٰهُ أَكْبَرُ اَللّٰهُ أَكْبَرُ

Q2: How can we bring اللهُ أَكْبَرُ into our lives?

Ans:

Q3: What is the message of أَشْهَدُ أَنْ لَّا إِلٰهَ إِلَّا اللهُ?

Ans:

Q4: What is the message of أَشْهَدُ أَنَّ مُحَمَّدًا رَّسُوْلُ اللهِ?

Ans:

Q5: What are the benefits in this world and in the Hereafter for those who offer prayers (Salah)?

Ans:

Q1: Translate the following.

اَلصَّلٰوةُ	خَيْرٌ	مِّنَ النَّوْمِ.

قَدْ	قَامَتِ	الصَّلَاةُ.

أَشْهَدُ	أَنْ	لَّا	إِلٰهَ	اِلَّا	اللهُ

وَحْدَهُ	لَا شَرِيْكَ	لَهُ

وَأَشْهَدُ	أَنَّ	مُحَمَّدًا	عَبْدُهُ	وَرَسُوْلُهُ.

اَللّٰهُمَّ	اجْعَلْنِي	مِنَ التَّوَّابِيْنَ	وَاجْعَلْنِي	مِنَ الْمُتَطَهِّرِيْنَ.

Q2: What do you say before you start Wudoo?
Ans:

Q3: What is the virtue/reward of reciting the Du'aa after Wudoo?
Ans:

Q4: What is the message of عَبْدُهُ in the du'aa of Wudoo?
Ans:

Q5: What is meant by neatness and purity?

Workbook

الْعَظِيمُ.	رَبِّيَ	سُبْحٰنَ

حَمِدَهُ.	لِمَنْ	سَمِعَ اللّٰهُ

الْحَمْدُ	وَلَكَ	رَبَّنَا	اللّٰهُمَّ

بَيْنَهُمَا،	وَمِلْءَ الْأَرْضِ وَمَا	مِلْءَ السَّمٰوٰتِ

بَعْدُ.	مِنْ شَيْءٍ	شِئْتَ	مَا	وَمِلْءَ

الْأَعْلٰى.	رَبِّيَ	سُبْحٰنَ

Q2: Write the four things we say to Allah during Rukoo'?
Ans:

Q3: Write the four things we say to Allah during Sajdah?
Ans:

Q4: What are the meanings of سُبْحٰن?
Ans:

Q5: Give 2 meanings of Hamd. What should our feelings be when we do Hamd?
Ans:

Q1: Translate the following.

اَلتَّحِيَّاتُ	لِلهِ	وَالصَّلَوَاتُ	وَالطَّيِّبَاتُ

اَلسَّلَامُ	عَلَيْكَ	أَيُّهَا النَّبِيُّ	وَرَحْمَةُ اللهِ	وَبَرَكَاتُهُ،

اَلسَّلَامُ	عَلَيْنَا	وَعَلَىٰ	عِبَادِ اللهِ	الصَّالِحِينَ،

أَشْهَدُ	أَنْ	لَّا إِلٰهَ	إِلَّا اللهُ

وَأَشْهَدُ أَنَّ	مُحَمَّدًا	عَبْدُهُ	وَرَسُولُهُ.

Q2: What should we do when we hear the three types of worship?
Ans:

Q3: Give examples of اَلتَّحِيَّات and اَلصَّلَوَات.
Ans:

Q4: How many favors are we asking Allah for the Prophet ﷺ?
Ans:

Q5: What is the message given in the word أَشْهَدُ here?
Ans:

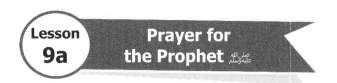

Q1: Translate the following.

مُحَمَّدٍ	وَّعَلىٰ الِ	عَلىٰ مُحَمَّدٍ	صَلِّ	اَللّٰهُمَّ

إِبْرَاهِيْمَ	وَعَلىٰ الِ	عَلىٰ إِبْرَاهِيْمَ	صَلَّيْتَ	كَمَا

مَّجِيْدٌ.	حَمِيْدٌ	إِنَّكَ

بَارَكْتَ	---	اَللّٰهُمَّ بَارِكْ

Q2: In order to recite the prayer for the Prophet ﷺ effectively, what can we remember?
Ans:

Q3: What are the meanings of صَلِّ عَلىٰ and بَارِك عَلىٰ?
Ans:

Q4: What reward is bestowed to Ibrahim (A.S) by Allah?
Ans:

Q5: Why Hameed and Majeed are mentioned at the end of this prayer?
Ans:

Q1: Translate the following.

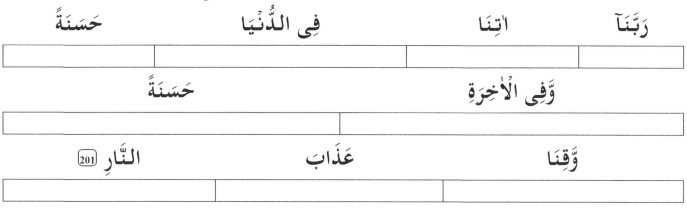

حَسَنَةً	فِى الدُّنْيَا	اٰتِنَا	رَبَّنَآ

حَسَنَةً	وَّفِى الْاٰخِرَةِ

النَّارِ ⟨201⟩	عَذَابَ	وَّقِنَا

Another supplication.

وَحُسْنِ عِبَادَتِكَ.	وَشُكْرِكَ	عَلٰى ذِكْرِكَ	أَعِنِّي	اَللّٰهُمَّ

Q2: What are the حَسَنَات of this world?

Ans:

Q3: What are the حَسَنَات of Aakhirah (the Hereafter)?

Ans:

Q4: What are the stages of purification for a sinner?

Ans:

Q5: Who taught the supplication (اَللّٰهُمَّ أَعِنِّي عَلٰى ذِكْرِكَ...) and to whom?

Ans:

Q1: Translate the following.

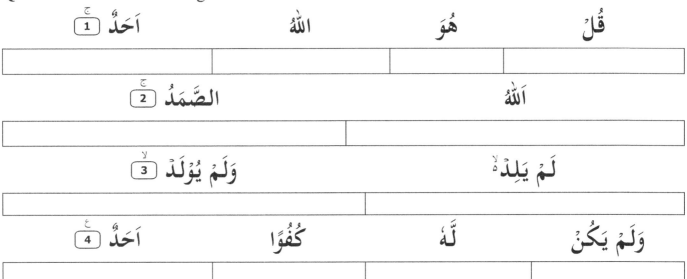

Q2: Write a few sentences about the virtues of Surah Al-Ikhlas?
Ans:

Q3: Write five things mentioned in this Surah about Allah?
Ans:

Q4: What is the meaning of "اَللّٰهُ الصَّمَدُ"؟
Ans:

Q5: Narrate the story of the companion of our Prophet ﷺ who loved this Surah?
Ans:

Q1: Translate the following.

قُلْ	اَعُوْذُ	بِرَبِّ	الْفَلَقِ ①

مِنْ شَرِّ	مَا	خَلَقَ ②	

وَمِنْ شَرِّ	غَاسِقٍ	اِذَا	وَقَبَ ③

وَمِنْ شَرِّ	النَّفّٰثٰتِ	فِى الْعُقَدِ ④	

وَمِنْ شَرِّ	حَاسِدٍ	اِذَا حَسَدَ ⑤	

Q2: Which Surahs did our prophet ﷺ recite after every obligatory prayer and before sleep?
Ans:

Q3: To recite this Surah effectively, what should we remember and realize?
Ans:

Q4: What evils happen in the night?
Ans:

Q5: Explain the meaning of "حَسَدَ".
Ans:

Q1: Translate the following.

Q2: Give the meanings of "رَبّ" with examples?

Ans:

Q3: Write the meanings of Sharr شَرّ (evil) and give its examples?

Ans:

Q4: How does Shaitaan whisper?

Ans:

Q5: How do the evil people whisper?

Ans:

Q1: Translate the following.

وَالْعَصْرِ ①	اِنَّ	الْاِنْسَانَ	لَفِيْ خُسْرٍ ②

اِلَّا	الَّذِيْنَ	اٰمَنُوْا	وَعَمِلُوا	الصّٰلِحٰتِ

وَتَوَاصَوْا	بِالْحَقِّ	وَتَوَاصَوْا	بِالصَّبْرِ ③

Q2: What is the message in the oath "By the Time"?
Ans:

Q3: What are the conditions for one to be safe from loss?
Ans:

Q4: Where do you find the truth?
Ans:

Q5: How many types of Sabr are there?
Ans:

Lesson 15a — Surah An-Nasr

Q1: Translate the following.

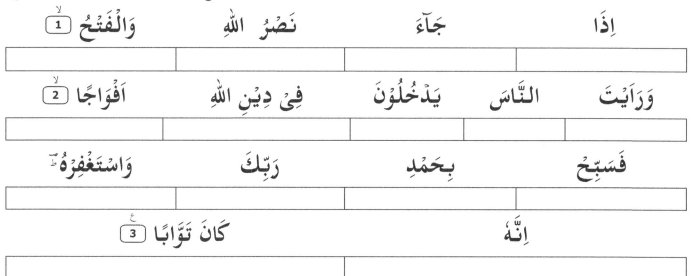

إِذَا	جَآءَ	نَصْرُ اللهِ	وَالْفَتْحُ ١

وَرَأَيْتَ	النَّاسَ	يَدْخُلُوْنَ	فِىْ دِيْنِ اللهِ	أَفْوَاجًا ٢

فَسَبِّحْ	بِحَمْدِ	رَبِّكَ	وَاسْتَغْفِرْهُ

اِنَّهُ	كَانَ تَوَّابًا ٣

Q2: When was this Surah revealed?
Ans:

Q3: Explain the difference between تَسْبِيح and حَمْد?
Ans:

Q4: Which victory is referred to in this Surah?
Ans:

Q5: What lessons do we get from Surah An-Nasr?
Ans:

Q1: Translate the following.

قُلْ	يَاَيُّهَا	الْكٰفِرُوْنَ ①

لَاۤ اَعْبُدُ	مَا	تَعْبُدُوْنَ ②

وَلَاۤ اَنْتُمْ	عٰبِدُوْنَ	مَاۤ	اَعْبُدُ ③

وَلَاۤ اَنَا	عَابِدٌ	مَّا	عَبَدْتُّمْ ④

وَلَاۤ اَنْتُمْ	عٰبِدُوْنَ	مَاۤ	اَعْبُدُ ⑤

لَكُمْ	دِيْنُكُمْ	وَلِىَ	دِيْنِ ⑥

Q2: Who were called as Kafiroon in this Surah and why?
Ans:

Q3: Do you think that لَكُمْ دِيْنُكُمْ وَلِىَ دِيْنِ means that we should stop propagating Islam? Why or why not?
Ans:

Q4: What are the meanings of عبادة?
Ans:

Q5: What are the benefits of reciting this Surah in the night?
Ans:

Q1: Translate the following.

كِتٰبٌ	اَنْزَلْنٰهُ	اِلَيْكَ	مُبٰرَكٌ

لِّيَدَّبَّرُوٓا	اٰيٰتِه	وَلِيَتَذَكَّرَ	اُولُوا الْاَلْبَابِ ۝

Q2: Explain the meaning of تَدَبُّر with an example.
Ans:

Q3: Explain the meaning of تَذَكُّر with an example.
Ans:

Q4: Describe the four dimensions of our relationship with the Quran.
Ans:

Q5: Describe different aspects of تَدَبُّر and simple steps to do تَذَكُّر.
Ans:

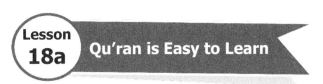
Q1: Translate the following:

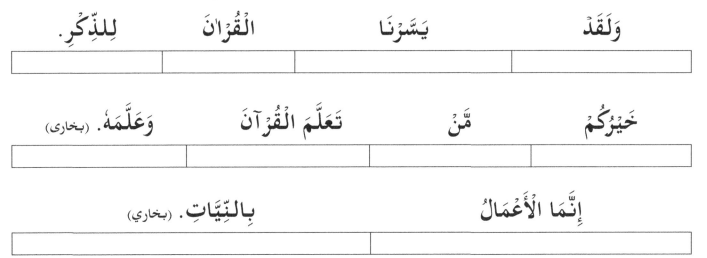

لِلذِّكْرِ.	الْقُرْاٰنَ	يَسَّرْنَا	وَلَقَدْ

وَعَلَّمَهُ. (بخارى)	تَعَلَّمَ الْقُرْآنَ	مَّنْ	خَيْرُكُمْ

بِالنِّيَّاتِ. (بخاري)	إِنَّمَا الْأَعْمَالُ

Q2: What are the meanings of Dhikr ?
Ans:

Q3: Give proofs that the Qur'an is easy to learn.
Ans:

Q4: Give examples of bad intention.
Ans:

Q5: Give the meanings and examples for إِنَّمَا ،إِنْ and إِنَّ.
Ans:

Lesson
19a
How to learn
the Qur'an?

Q1: Translate the following.

(طه: 114) عِلْمًا ١١٤	زِدْنِىْ	رَبِّ

(العلق:4) بِالْقَلَمِ	عَلَّمَ	الَّذِىْ

(الملك: 2) عَمَلًا ۚ	اَحْسَنُ	اَيُّكُمْ

Q2: In what ways is increase in knowledge beneficial?
Ans:

Q3: What efforts can you make after asking Allah for knowledge?
Ans:

Q4: What was the first order given to Prophet ﷺ in the first revelation?
Ans:

Q5: In what areas should we try to be the best and compete with each other?
 Ans:

Q1: Write meanings in the empty boxes which you learned in previous 19 lessons.

لِّلْمُتَّقِيْنَ ٢   هُدًى   فِيْهِ   لَارَيْبَ   الْكِتٰبُ   ذٰلِكَ   الٓمّٓ ١

رَزَقْنٰهُمْ   وَمِمَّا   الصَّلٰوةَ   وَيُقِيْمُوْنَ   بِالْغَيْبِ   يُؤْمِنُوْنَ   الَّذِيْنَ

وَمَآ   اِلَيْكَ   اُنْزِلَ   بِمَآ   يُؤْمِنُوْنَ   وَالَّذِيْنَ   ٣   يُنْفِقُوْنَ

يُوْقِنُوْنَ ٤   هُمْ   وَبِالْاٰخِرَةِ   مِنْ قَبْلِكَ   اُنْزِلَ

رَّبِّهِمْ   مِّنْ   هُدًى   عَلٰى   اُولٰٓئِكَ

الْمُفْلِحُوْنَ ٥   هُمْ   وَاُولٰٓئِكَ

Q1: Write the six Arabic words that you have learnt for "He, they, …" in the first column. Write the same six words starting with وَ in the second column and with "فَ" in the third column.

Q2: Break the Arabic words and write the meanings.	
فَهُمْ	
وَنَحْنُ	
وَهُوَ	
وَأَنْتُمْ	
وَأَنْتَ	

Q3: Translate the following into Arabic.	
They	
So I	
And you all	
So he	
And we	

Q4: Answer the following questions in Arabic.	
مَنْ أَنْتَ؟	
مَنْ أَنْتُمْ؟	
مَنْ هُمْ؟	
مَنْ هُوَ؟	
مَنْ مُحَمَّدٌ صلى الله عليه وسلم؟	

هُوَ مُسْلِم، هُمْ مُسْلِمُون...

Q1: Make plural of the following nouns adding "ون" and "ين".		
واحد	Plural with ـون	Plural with ـين
مُؤْمِن		
صالِح		
مُشْرِك		
مُسْلِم		
كَافِر		

Q2: Break the Arabic words and write the meanings.	
فَأَنْتَ صَالِح	
مِنْ مُشْرِك	
وَهُوَ مُؤْمِن	
وَأَنْتُمْ مُسْلِمُوْن	
وَهُمْ صَالِحُوْن	

Q3: Translate the following into Arabic.	
He is a believer	
We are Muslims	
And he is righteous	
They are righteous	
You are a believer	

Q4: Answer the following questions in Arabic.	
مَنْ أَنْتُمْ؟	
هَلْ أَنْتُمْ مُؤْمِنُوْن؟	
مَنْ هُوَ؟	
هَلْ أَنْتَ صَالِح؟	
هَلْ هُمْ مُؤْمِنُوْن؟	

Q1: Fill up the following table by attaching ــهُ، ـهُمْ، ـهُ etc. to the words رَبّ،
دِيْن and كِتَاب . The first row is filled up for your ease.

كِتَابُهُ	دِيْنُهُ	رَبُّهُ

Q2: Break the Arabic words and write their meanings.

دِيْنُكُمْ	
وَهُوَ رَبُّنَا	
دِيْنُهُمْ	
رَبُّكُمْ	
اَللهُ رَبُّهُمْ	

Q3: Translate the following into Arabic.

His Lord	
And our Lord	
Their religion	
Your religion	
My pen	

Q4: Answer the following questions in Arabic.

مَنْ رَبُّكَ؟	
مَنْ رَسُوْلُهُمْ؟	
مَا دِيْنُهُ؟	
مَنْ رَبُّهُمْ؟	
مَا دِيْنُكُمْ؟	

Q1: Write the feminine gender of the following nouns and write their plurals too.

Masculine gender	Feminine gender (singular)	Feminine gender (plural)
صَالِح		
كَافِر		
مُؤْمِن		
عَالِم		
مُسْلِم		

Q2: Break the Arabic words and write the meanings.	
مَنْ رَبُّهَا؟	
هِيَ صَالِحَة	
قَلَمُهَا	
وَهِيَ مُؤْمِنَة	
فَهِيَ مُسْلِمَة	

Q3: Translate the following into Arabic.	
She is a Muslim.	
We are righteous women.	
Her book	
Her pen	
She is a believer.	

Q4: Answer the following questions in Arabic.	
مَا دِيْنُهَا؟	
مَنْ هِيَ؟	
مَا كِتَابُهَا؟	
هَلْ هِيَ مُسْلِمَة؟	
مَا كِتَابُهُمْ؟	

Q1: Translate the following into Arabic using the words that you learnt in Lesson 5b.

for him	from him	with him
for them	from them	with them
for you	from you	with you
for I	from me	with me
for you all	from you all	with you all
for us	from us	with us

Q2: Break the Arabic words and write the meanings.

رَضِيَ اللهُ عَنْهُمْ	
وَمِنْكُمْ	
مِنَ الرَّسُوْلِ	
اَلْكِتَابُ لَهَا	
هٰذَا لَكُمْ	

Q3: Translate the following into Arabic.

For her	
From you all	
And from me	
For us	
So from them	

Q4: Answer the following using "نَعَمْ".

أَهٰذَا لَكَ؟	
أَهٰذَا مِنْكُمْ؟	
أَهٰذَا لِيْ؟	
أَذٰلِكَ لَهُمْ؟	
أَهٰذَا لَهَا؟	

Q1: Translate the following into Arabic using the words that you learnt in Lesson 6b.

in him	in him	on him
in them	in them	on them
in you	in you	on you
in me	in me	on me
in you all	in you all	on you all
in us	in us	on us

Q2: Break the Arabic words and write the meanings.

اَلسَّلَامُ عَلَيْكُمْ	
هٰذَا فِى الْكِتَابِ	
مَنْ فِى الْبَيْتِ؟	
رَحْمَةُ اللهِ عَلَيْهَا	
بِسْمِ اللهِ	

Q3: Translate the following into Arabic.

In the masjid	
On her	
on the book	
From the Qur'an	
From us	

Q4: Answer the following in Arabic using "نَعَمْ".

هَلْ فِيْكَ خَيْرٌ؟	
هَلْ فِيْهِمْ خَيْرٌ؟	
هَلْ فِيْكُمْ خَيْرٌ؟	
هَلْ فِيْهِ خَيْرٌ؟	
هَلْ فِيْهَا خَيْرٌ؟	

Q1: Translate the following into Arabic using the words that you learnt in Lesson 7b.

with / near him	with him	to him
with / near them	with them	to them
with / near you	with you	to you
with / near me	with me	to me
with / near you all	with you all	to you all
with / near us	with us	to us

Q2: Break the Arabic words and write the meanings.

اَللهُ مَعَنَا	
عِنْدَ اللهِ	
رَضِيَ اللهُ عَنْهَا	
هَلِ الْقُرْآنُ مَعَهَا؟	
إِلَى اللهِ	

Q3: Translate the following into Arabic.

Towards Islam	
Allah is with you all.	
Near the house	
Is the book with you?	
They all are with us.	

Q4: Answer the following in Arabic using "نَعَمْ".

هَلِ اللهُ مَعَكُمْ؟	
هَلْ عِنْدَهُ كِتَابٌ؟	
هَلْ عِنْدَكَ قَلَمٌ؟	
هَلِ اللهُ مَعَكَ؟	
هَلِ الْكِتَابُ مَعَكَ؟	

Q1: Write the following words "this, these, that, those, this (feminine)" in Arabic in the first column. And write them with وَ and فَ in the 2nd and 3rd column.

Q2: Break the Arabic words and write their meanings.

فَأُولٰئِكَ مَعَ الْمُؤْمِنِينَ	
هٰؤُلَاءِ لَضَآلُّونَ	
هٰذَا مِنْ عِنْدِ اللهِ	
أُولٰئِكَ هُمُ الْمُؤْمِنُوْنَ	
ذٰلِكَ الْكِتٰبُ	

Q3: Translate the following into Arabic.

This is a book.	
They are Muslims.	
Towards them	
He is righteous.	
These are believers.	

Q4: Answer the following in Arabic using "نَعَمْ".

أَهٰؤُلَاءِ مُسْلِمُوْنَ؟	
أَهٰذَا مُؤْمِنٌ؟	
أَذٰلِكَ مُسْلِمٌ؟	
هَلْ أُولٰئِكَ صَابِرُوْنَ؟	
أَهٰذِهِ صَالِحَةٌ؟	

Q1: Complete the following table with the six forms of فعل ماض for the verbs فعل، فتح، جعل that you have learnt in Lesson 9b.

Q2: Break the Arabic words and write the meanings.

اَلَّذِىْ جَعَلَ لَكُمْ	
فَجَعَلْنَا لَهُ	
فَتَحَ لِيْ	
إِنَّا فَتَحْنَا لَكَ	
فَجَعَلْتُمْ مِنْهُ	

Q3: Translate the following into Arabic.

We opened the book.	
I made for him	
we opened for you	
we made for you	
They made for you all	

Q4: Answer the following in Arabic using "نَعَمْ".

هَلْ جَعَلَ؟	
هَلْ جَعَلْتَ؟	
هَلْ جَعَلْتُمْ؟	
هَلْ فَتَحْتُمْ؟	

فعل ماضٍ: نَصَرَ، خَلَقَ، ذَكَرَ، عَبَدَ

Q1: Complete the following table with the six forms of فعل ماض for the verbs نصر، عبد، خلق، ذكر that you have learnt in Lesson 10b.

Q2: Break the Arabic words and write the meanings.	
وَلَقَدْ نَصَرَكُمُ اللهُ	
وَذَكَرُوا اللهَ	
لَقَدْ خَلَقْنَا الْإِنْسَانَ	
مَا عَبَدْنَاهُمْ	
فَقَدْ نَصَرَهُ اللهُ	

Q3: Translate the following into Arabic.	
We helped Zaid.	
You all worshipped Allah	
He created the man	
You all remembered Allah	
I worshipped Allah	

Q4: Answer the following in Arabic using "نَعَمْ".	
	هَلْ نَصَرُوا مَحْمُودًا؟
	هَلْ خَلَقْتُمْ شَيْئًا؟
	هَلْ ذَكَرَ الرَّحْمٰنَ؟
	هَلْ عَبَدَتِ اللهَ؟
	هَلْ نَصَرْتَ النَّاسَ؟

Q1: Complete the following table with the six forms of فعل ماض for the verbs ضرب، سمع، علم، عمل that you have learnt in Lesson 11b.

<table>
<tr><td colspan="2">Q2: Break the Arabic words and write the meanings.</td></tr>
<tr><td>مَنْ ضَرَبَ سَعْدًا؟</td><td></td></tr>
<tr><td>اَلَّذِيْنَ سَمِعُوا الْقُرْآنَ</td><td></td></tr>
<tr><td>وَلَقَدْ عَلِمْتُمُ الرَّسُوْلَ</td><td></td></tr>
<tr><td>لَقَدْ سَمِعَ اللهُ</td><td></td></tr>
<tr><td>اَلَّذِيْنَ سَمِعُوْا وَعَمِلُوْا</td><td></td></tr>
</table>

<table>
<tr><td colspan="2">Q3: Translate the following into Arabic.</td></tr>
<tr><td>Did you listen to the Qur'an?</td><td></td></tr>
<tr><td>They did not beat/hit Zaid</td><td></td></tr>
<tr><td>We did righteous deed</td><td></td></tr>
<tr><td>I knew Islam</td><td></td></tr>
<tr><td>She did good deeds</td><td></td></tr>
</table>

Q4: Answer the following in Arabic using "نَعَمْ".

هَلْ عَلِمْتَ الْحَدِيْثَ؟	
هَلْ سَمِعْتُمُ الْقُرْآنَ؟	
هَلْ عَمِلَ صَالِحًا؟	
هَلْ عَمِلْتَ صَالِحًا؟	
هَلْ سَمِعْتَ تِلَاوَةَ الْقُرْآنِ؟	

فعل مضارع: يَفْعَلُ، يَجْعَلُ، يَفْتَحُ

Q1: Complete the following table with the six forms of فعل مضارع for the verbs فعل، جعل، فتح that you have learnt in Lesson 12b.

Q2: Break the Arabic words and write the meanings.	
مَنْ يَّفْعَلُ ذٰلِكَ؟	
اَتَجْعَلُ فِيهَا؟	
اَللّٰهُ يَجْعَلُ فِيهِ خَيْرًا	
اَلَّذِي يَجْعَلُ لَكُمْ	
تَفْتَحُوْنَ الْكِتَابَ	

Q3: Translate the following into Arabic.	
I do good deeds	
We make for him	
Do you open the book?	
He made for you	
She opens the book	

Q4: Answer the following in Arabic using "نَعَمْ".	
هَلْ تَجْعَلُ؟	
هَلْ تَفْتَحُ الْكِتَابَ؟	
هَلْ تَجْعَلُونَ الْبَيْتَ؟	
هَلْ يَجْعَلُ شَيْئًا؟	
هَلْ تَفْعَلُوْنَ خَيْرًا؟	

فعل مضارع: يَنْصُرُ، يَخْلُقُ، يَذْكُرُ، يَعْبُدُ

Q1: Complete the following table with the six forms of فعل مضارع for the verbs نصر، خلق، ذكر، عبد that you have learnt in Lesson 13b.

Q2: Break the Arabic words and write the meanings.		**Q3:** Translate the following into Arabic.	
مَنْ يَّنْصُرُهُ؟		And he helps Zaid	
لَا يَخْلُقُونَ شَيْئًا		And he creates men	
اَلَّذِينَ يَذْكُرُونَ اللهَ		They all remember Allah	
مَنْ يَّعْبُدُ اللهَ؟		You worship Allah	
لَا يَعْبُدُونَ غَيْرَ اللهِ		She will help Khalid	

Q4: Answer the following in Arabic using "نَعَمْ".	
هَلْ تَعْبُدُونَ اللهَ؟	
هَلْ تَعْبُدُ اللهَ؟	
هَلِ اللهُ يَخْلُقُنَا؟	
هَلْ يَنْصُرُونَ خَالِدًا؟	
هَلْ تَذْكُرُونَ الرَّحْمٰنَ؟	

فعل مضارع: يَضْرِبُ، يَسْمَعُ، يَعْلَمُ، يَعْمَلُ

Q1: Complete the following table with the six forms of فعل مضارع for the verbs
ضرب، سمع، علم، عمل that you have learnt in Lesson 14b.

Q2: Break the Arabic words and write the meanings.

اَلنَّاسُ يَضْرِبُوْنَ	
وَأَنْتُمْ تَسْمَعُوْنَ الْقُرْاٰنَ	
إِنَّهُ يَعْلَمُ الْخَيْرَ والشَّرَّ	
اَللهُ يَعْلَمُ مَا تَعْمَلُوْنَ	
لَا يَسْمَعُوْنَ فِيهَا	

Q3: Translate the following into Arabic.

He does not beat/hit	
They listen to Al-Qur'an	
Do you all know Zaid?	
You all do good deeds	
They all act on this	

Q4: Answer the following in Arabic using "نَعَمْ".

هَلْ تَضْرِبُ زَيْدًا؟	
هَلْ تَسْمَعُ الْقُرْاٰنَ فِى الصَّلَاةِ؟	
هَلْ تَعْمَلُ صَالِحًا؟	
هَلِ اللهُ يَعْلَمُ مَا تَعْمَلُوْنَ؟	
هَلْ تَعْلَمُ النَّاسَ؟	

Q1: Complete the following table for the verbs فتح and جعل similar to what is done for فعل.

		اِفْعَلْ
		اِفْعَلُوا
		لَا تَفْعَلْ
		لَا تَفْعَلُوا

Q2: Break the Arabic words and write the meanings.

فَافْعَلْ خَيْرًا!	
اِفْتَحِ الْكِتَابَ!	
وَافْعَلُوا الْخَيْرَ!	
وَلَا تَجْعَلُوا!	
لَا تَفْعَلُوا شَرًّا!	

Q3: Translate the following into Arabic.

You all do good work	
You don't open	
You all don't do evil deeds	
You all open the book	
You don't make anything	

Q4: Answer the following in Arabic.

اِفْعَلُوا خَيْرًا!	
اِجْعَلْ!	
اِفْتَحُوا الْكِتَابَ!	
اِفْعَلْ خَيْرًا!	
اِفْتَحِ الْكِتَابَ!	

Q1: Complete the following table using what you learnt in Lesson 16b.

			اُنْصُرْ
	اُعْبُدُوْا		
		لَا تَذْكُرْ	
لَا تَخْلُقُوْا			

Q2: Break the Arabic words and write the meanings.

اُذْكُرُوْا اٰيَةَ الْقُرْاٰنِ!	
اُعْبُدُوْا رَبَّكُمْ!	
لَا تَنْصُرْ ظَالِمًا!	
وَانْصُرُوْا زَيْدًا!	
اُذْكُرْ رَبَّكَ!	

Q3: Translate the following into Arabic.

You all remember Allah	
You remember Rahman	
You all worship Allah	
You all don't help the wrongdoer	
You all help Zaid	

Q4: Answer the following in Arabic.

اُعْبُدِ اللّٰهَ!	
اُعْبُدُوا اللّٰهَ!	
اُذْكُرِ الرَّحْمٰنَ!	
اُنْصُرْ وَلَدًا!	
اُذْكُرُوا اللّٰهَ!	

Q1: Complete the following table using what you learnt in Lesson 17b.

			اِضْرِب
اِعْمَلُوا			
		لَا تَسْمَعْ	
	لَا تَعْلَمُوا		

Q2: Break the Arabic words and write the meanings.

لَا تَضْرِبُوا زَيْدًا!	
لَا تَسْمَعُوا شَرًّا!	
وَاسْمَعْ تِلَاوَةَ الْقُرْاٰنِ!	
وَاعْلَمُوا أَنَّ اللهَ رَحِيمٌ!	
وَاعْمَلُوا صَالِحًا!	

Q3: Translate the following into Arabic.

Listen (all of you) to the Qur'an	
Don't do wrong!	
Do (all of you) good work!	
Don't (all of you) beat Zaid!	
And you all know	

Q4: Answer the following in Arabic.

اِعْلَمِ الْحَدِيْثَ!	
اِسْمَعُوا الْقُرْاٰنَ!	
اِضْرِبِ الظَّالِمَ!	
لَا تَعْمَلُوا شَرًّا!	
اِعْمَلُوا الصَّالِحَاتِ!	

اسم فاعل، اسم مفعول، **Name of action**:
فَعَلَ، فَتَحَ، جَعَلَ...

Active participle, passive participle & Masdar

Q1: Write the Active participle, passive participle & Masdar with plurals of the verbs given below.

نَصَرَ	جَعَلَ	فَتَحَ	فَعَلَ
			فَاعِل
			مَفْعُوْل
			فِعل
			فَاعِلُوْن، فَاعِلِيْن
			مَفْعُوْلُوْنَ، مَفْعُوْلِيْن

<table>
<tr><td colspan="2">

Q2: Break the Arabic words and write the meanings.

</td><td colspan="2">

Q3: Translate the following into Arabic.

</td></tr>
</table>

اِنِّىْ فَاعِلٌ ذٰلِكَ	
أَنْتُمْ فَاعِلُوْن	
أَنْتَ فَاتِح	
اَلْمُسْلِمُوْنَ مَنْصُوْرُوْن	
اَلْكِتَابُ مَفْتُوْح	

You are the openers	
Masjid is opened	
Believers are the doers	
We are being helped	
I am doer.	

Q4: Answer the following in Arabic using "نَعَمْ".

هَلْ أَنْتَ فَاعِل؟	
هَلِ الْمَدْرَسَةُ مَفْتُوْحَة؟	
هَلْ أَنْتَ نَاصِر؟	
هَلْ أَنْتُمْ جَاعِلُوْنَ؟	
هَلْ هِيَ فَاعِلَة؟	

Lesson
19b

اسم فاعل، اسم مفعول، Name of action:
عَبَدَ، ضَرَبَ، سَمِعَ...

Q1: Write the Active participle, passive participle & Masdar with plurals of the verbs given below.

عَمِلَ	عَلِمَ	سَمِعَ	ضَرَبَ	عَبَدَ
				عَابِد
				مَعْبُوْد
				عِبَادَة
				عَابِدُوْن، عَابِدِيْن
				مَعْبُوْدُوْن،مَعْبُوْدِيْن

Q2: Break the Arabic words and write the meanings.

عِلْمُهَا عِنْدَ رَبِّي	
لِى عَمَلِيْ وَلَكُمْ عَمَلُكُمْ	
وَنَحْنُ لَهُ عٰبِدُوْنَ	
فَاعْمَلْ اِنَّنَا عٰمِلُوْنَ	
وَالذَّاكِرُوْنَ اللهَ كَثِيْرًا	

Q3: Translate the following into Arabic.

We are the listeners	
We are the doers.	
Indeed Allah is the knower.	
The Salah is a worship.	
She is a worshipper.	

Q4: Answer the following in Arabic using "نَعَمْ".

هَلِ اللهُ مَعْبُوْدُنَا؟	
هَلْ هُمْ عَالِمُوْنَ؟	
هَلْ أَنْتَ عَامِلٌ خَيْرًا؟	
هَلْ عِنْدَكُمْ مِنْ عِلْمٍ؟	
هَلْ هٰذَا الْعَمَلُ الصَّالِحُ؟	

Q1: Write the short table of the verbs given below.

فعل	مفعول	فاعل	نهي	أمر	مضارع	ماضٍ
						فَعَلَ
						ضَرَبَ
						سَمِعَ
						خَلَقَ
						ذَكَرَ

Q2: Write the following forms joined with attached pronouns.

ذَكَرَتَهُ	يَسْمَعُهُ	يَعْلَمُهُ	يَنْصُرُهُ
ذَكَرَتْهُمْ	يَسْمَعُهُمْ	يَعْلَمُهُمْ	يَنْصُرُهُمْ

Q4: Answer the following in Arabic using "نَعَمْ".

	هَلْ تَنْصُرُنِي؟
	هَلْ تَسْمَعُونَنَا؟
	هَلْ ذَكَرْتَنِي؟
	هَلْ تَعْلَمُونَهُ؟
	هَلْ سَمِعْتَنِي؟

Arabic text used in this course (for a quick review)

1- Ta'awwuz: أَعُوذُ بِاللهِ مِنَ الشَّيْطٰنِ الرَّجِيمِ

2 to 4. Surah Al-Fatihah:

بِسْمِ اللهِ الرَّحْمٰنِ الرَّحِيمِ ۝١ اَلْحَمْدُ للهِ رَبِّ الْعٰلَمِينَ ۝٢

الرَّحْمٰنِ الرَّحِيمِ ۝٣ مٰلِكِ يَوْمِ الدِّينِ ۝٤ اِيَّاكَ نَعْبُدُ وَاِيَّاكَ

نَسْتَعِينُ ۝٥ اِهْدِنَا الصِّرَاطَ الْمُسْتَقِيمَ ۝٦ صِرَاطَ الَّذِينَ

اَنْعَمْتَ عَلَيْهِمْ غَيْرِ الْمَغْضُوبِ عَلَيْهِمْ وَلَا الضَّآلِّينَ ۝٧

5-Adhaan: اَللهُ أَكْبَرُ   اَللهُ أَكْبَرُ   اَللهُ أَكْبَرُ   اَللهُ أَكْبَرُ

أَشْهَدُ أَنْ لَّا إِلٰهَ إِلَّا اللهُ، أَشْهَدُ أَنَّ مُحَمَّدًا رَّسُولُ اللهِ

حَيَّ عَلَى الصَّلٰوةِ ❋ حَيَّ عَلَى الْفَلَاحِ

اَللهُ أَكْبَرُ   اَللهُ أَكْبَرُ ❋ لَا إِلٰهَ إِلَّا اللهُ

6- Extra in Fajr Adhaan: اَلصَّلٰوةُ خَيْرٌ مِّنَ النَّوْمِ

Extra in Iqamah: .قَدْ قَامَتِ الصَّلَاةُ

After Wudoo:

أَشْهَدُ أَنْ لَّا إِلٰهَ إِلَّا اللهُ وَحْدَهُ لَا شَرِيكَ لَهُ

وَأَشْهَدُ أَنَّ مُحَمَّدًا عَبْدُهُ وَرَسُولُهُ،

اَللّٰهُمَّ اجْعَلْنِي مِنَ التَّوَّابِينَ وَاجْعَلْنِي مِنَ الْمُتَطَهِّرِينَ.

7-Rukoo', Sujood

سُبْحٰنَ رَبِّيَ الْعَظِيمِ،

سَمِعَ اللهُ لِمَنْ حَمِدَهُ،   رَبَّنَا وَلَكَ الْحَمْدُ.

مِلْءَ السَّمٰوَاتِ وَمِلْءَ الْأَرْضِ وَمِلْءَ مَا بَيْنَهُمَا

وَمِلْءَ مَا شِئْتَ مِنْ شَيْءٍ بَعْدُ.

سُبْحٰنَ رَبِّيَ الْأَعْلٰى

8- Tashah-hud

اَلتَّحِيَّاتُ للهِ وَالصَّلَوَاتُ وَالطَّيِّبَاتُ،

اَلسَّلَامُ عَلَيْكَ اَيُّهَا النَّبِيُّ وَرَحْمَةُ اللهِ وَبَرَكَاتُهُ،

اَلسَّلَامُ عَلَيْنَا وَعَلٰى عِبَادِ اللهِ الصّٰلِحِينَ،

أَشْهَدُ أَنْ لَّا إِلٰهَ إِلَّا اللهُ وَأَشْهَدُ أَنَّ مُحَمَّدًا عَبْدُهُ وَرَسُولُهُ.

9- Prayer for the Prophet ﷺ

اَللّٰهُمَّ صَلِّ عَلٰى مُحَمَّدٍ وَّعَلٰى اٰلِ مُحَمَّدٍ كَمَا صَلَّيْتَ عَلٰى

إِبْرَاهِيمَ وَعَلٰى اٰلِ إِبْرَاهِيمَ إِنَّكَ حَمِيدٌ مَّجِيدٌ.

اَللّٰهُمَّ بَارِكْ عَلٰى مُحَمَّدٍ وَّعَلٰى اٰلِ مُحَمَّدٍ كَمَا بَارَكْتَ عَلٰى

إِبْرَاهِيمَ وَعَلٰى اٰلِ إِبْرَاهِيمَ إِنَّكَ حَمِيدٌ مَّجِيدٌ.

10-Prayers after Salah

رَبَّنَآ اٰتِنَا فِى الدُّنْيَا حَسَنَةً وَّفِى الْأٰخِرَةِ حَسَنَةً

وَّقِنَا عَذَابَ النَّارِ.

اَللّٰهُمَّ أَعِنِّي عَلٰى ذِكْرِكَ وَشُكْرِكَ وَحُسْنِ عِبَادَتِكَ.

11- Surah Al-Ikhlas

قُلْ هُوَ اللهُ أَحَدٌ ۝١ اَللهُ الصَّمَدُ ۝٢

لَمْ يَلِدْ وَلَمْ يُولَدْ ۝٣ وَلَمْ يَكُنْ لَّهُ كُفُوًا أَحَدٌ ۝٤

12- Surah Al-Falaq:

قُلْ أَعُوذُ بِرَبِّ الْفَلَقِ ۝١ مِنْ شَرِّ مَا خَلَقَ ۝٢

وَمِنْ شَرِّ غَاسِقٍ إِذَا وَقَبَ ۝٣ وَمِنْ شَرِّ النَّفّٰثٰتِ فِى الْعُقَدِ

۝٤ وَمِنْ شَرِّ حَاسِدٍ إِذَا حَسَدَ ۝٥

13- Surah An-Naas

قُلْ أَعُوذُ بِرَبِّ النَّاسِ ۝١ مَلِكِ النَّاسِ ۝٢ اِلٰهِ النَّاسِ ۝٣

مِنْ شَرِّ الْوَسْوَاسِ الْخَنَّاسِ ۝٤ الَّذِي يُوَسْوِسُ فِى صُدُورِ

النَّاسِ ۝٥ مِنَ الْجِنَّةِ وَالنَّاسِ ۝٦

14- Surah Al-Asr

وَالْعَصْرِ ۝١ إِنَّ الْإِنْسَانَ لَفِى خُسْرٍ ۝٢ إِلَّا الَّذِينَ اٰمَنُوا

وَعَمِلُوا الصّٰلِحٰتِ وَتَوَاصَوْا بِالْحَقِّ وَتَوَاصَوْا بِالصَّبْرِ ۝٣

15- Surah An-Nasr

إِذَا جَآءَ نَصْرُ اللهِ وَالْفَتْحُ ۝١

وَرَأَيْتَ النَّاسَ يَدْخُلُونَ فِى دِينِ اللهِ أَفْوَاجًا ۝٢

فَسَبِّحْ بِحَمْدِ رَبِّكَ وَاسْتَغْفِرْهُ إِنَّهُ كَانَ تَوَّابًا ۝٣

16- Surah Al-Kafiroon

قُلْ يَآأَيُّهَا الْكٰفِرُونَ ۝١ لَا أَعْبُدُ مَا تَعْبُدُونَ ۝٢ وَلَآ أَنْتُمْ

عٰبِدُونَ مَا أَعْبُدُ ۝٣ وَلَآ أَنَا عَابِدٌ مَّا عَبَدْتُّمْ ۝٤ وَلَآ أَنْتُمْ

عٰبِدُونَ مَا أَعْبُدُ ۝٥ لَكُمْ دِينُكُمْ وَلِيَ دِينِ ۝٦

17- Purpose of revelation

كِتٰبٌ اَنْزَلْنٰهُ اِلَيْكَ مُبٰرَكٌ لِّيَدَّبَّرُوٓا اٰيٰتِهِ

وَلِيَتَذَكَّرَ أُولُوا الْأَلْبَابِ ۝٢٩

Tableegh (conveying):

بَلِّغُوا عَنِّي وَلَوْ اٰيَةً.

18-Qu'ran is easy to learn

وَلَقَدْ يَسَّرْنَا الْقُرْاٰنَ لِلذِّكْرِ (القمر:40)

خَيْرُكُمْ مَّنْ تَعَلَّمَ الْقُرْاٰنَ وَعَلَّمَهُ. (بخارى)

إِنَّمَا الْأَعْمَالُ بِالنِّيَّاتِ. (بخارى)

19- How to learn the Qur'an

❶ Ask Allah for knowledge.

رَبِّ زِدْنِي عِلْمًا.

❷ Use all resources: اَلَّذِي عَلَّمَ بِالْقَلَمِ

❸ Compete: اَيُّكُمْ أَحْسَنُ عَمَلًا

Understand Al-Quran & Salah – the Easy Way (Course-1)

Learn the message of Salah as well as the basic Arabic grammar at www.understandquran.com

The list has 232 words from Surah Al-Fatihah, last 6 Surahs, and Salah recitations. These words occur in the Qur'an more than 40,000 times (50% Of Qur'anic words). This is the best list to start learning Qur'an because you know the Arabic words, and you repeat them every day.

Beg Allah to help you study this regularly. Keep it always with you till you have memorized the meanings of all the words.

Start here↓

Column 1

1: INTRODUCTION & Ta'awwuz

7	أَعُوذُ	I seek refuge
2550	بِاللہ	in Allah
2471	مِنْ	from
88	شَيْطٰن، شَيَاطِين	Satan
6	الرَّجِيم	the outcast

— Grammar —

481	هُوَ	he
444	هُمْ	they
81	أَنْتَ	you
135	أَنَا	I
68	أَنْتُمْ	you all
86	نَحْنُ	we
831	مَنْ	who?

2: SURAH AL-FATIHAH (1-3)

39	اسْم، أَسْمَاء	the name
57	الرَّحْمٰن	the most gracious
115	الرَّحِيم	the most merciful
27	كَرِيم	Good mannered
43	الْحَمْد	All the praises and thanks
149	لله	be to Allah
199	رَب	Rabb
73	الْعٰلَمِين	(of) the worlds

— Grammar —

To make plural forms, add: ـــون، ـــين
Plural form of مُسْلِم is مُسْلِمُون or مُسْلِمِين

230	مُؤْمِن	a believer
49	مُشْرِك	a polytheist
134	كَافِر، كَافِرُون	a disbeliever
136	صَالِح	a pious person

3: SURAH AL-FATIHAH (4-5)

3	مَلِك	Master
405	يَوْم	the day
92	الدِّين	judgment
24	إِيَّاكَ	You alone
	نَعْبُد	we worship
1	نَسْتَعِين	we ask for help

— Grammar —

رَب This word occurred 772 times in the Qur'an (with different demonstrative nouns)

	رَبُّهُ	his Rabb

Column 2

	رَبُّهُمْ	their Rabb
	رَبُّكَ	your Rabb
	رَبِّى	my Rabb
	رَبُّكُمْ	your Rabb
	رَبُّنَا	our Rabb
2154	مَا	what?

4: SURAH AL-FATIHAH (6-7)

2	اهْدِنَا	Guide us
45	الصِّرَاط	(to) the path
37	الْمُسْتَقِيم	the straight
1080	الَّذِين	those
5	أَنْعَمْت	You (have) bestowed favors
216	عَلَيْهِم	on them
147	غَيْر	not
	الْمَغْضُوب	those who earned wrath
1687	وَلَا	and nor
14	الضَّالِّين	those who go astray

— Grammar —

64	هِيَ	she
	رَبُّهَا	her Rabb
	مُسْلِمَة	A muslim (fg, sl)
	مُسْلِمَات	muslim (fg, pl)

5: AZAAN

23	أَكْبَر	Greatest
1	أَشْهَدُ	I bear witness
571	أَنْ	that
359	أَنَّ	that
4	مُحَمَّد	Muhammad ﷺ
332	رَسُول، رُسُل	the messenger
	حَيَّ	Come!
83	الصَّلٰوة	the Salah
	الْفَلَاح	the prosperity
39	كَبِير	great
63	كَثِير	more
88	أَكْثَر	the most

— Grammar —

1361	لَ+ﻩ، هُم...	for
744	مِنْ+ﻩ، هُم...	from
416	عَنْ+ﻩ، هُم...	with

Column 3

6: FAJR AZAN, IQAMAH...

176	خَيْر	better
3	نَوْم	sleep
	قَد	certainly
40	شَرِيك شُرَكَاء	partner

— — — — Grammar — — — —

510	بِ+ﻩ، هُم...	with, in
1684	فِى+ﻩ، هُم...	in
1207	عَلٰى+ﻩ، هُم...	on
176	سَبِيل، سُبُل	path

7: RUKU & SUJOOD PRAYERS

41	سُبْحٰن	Glory
107	الْعَظِيم	the Magnificent
1	مِلْء	filling
461	أَرْض	t earth
310	سَمَاء، سَمٰوَات	sky
266	بَيْن	between
3	شِئْت	you will
283	شَيْء، أَشْيَاء	thing
198	بَعْد	after
11	عَلِيّ	high
9	أَعْلٰى	the highest

— Grammar —

736	إِلٰى+ﻩ، هُم	to, toward
163	مَعَ+ﻩ، هُم...	with
197	عِنْد+ﻩ، هُم...	with
4	رَاجِعُون	those who return
21	كَمْ	How many?

8: TASHAH-HUD

6	التَّحِيَّات	all worships of the tongue
	الصَّلَوَات	all worships of body
46	الطَّيِّبَات	all worships by spending wealth
42	السَّلٰم	peace
75	النَّبِى، أَنْبِيَاء، نَبِيُّون	prophet
114	رَحْمَة	mercy
3	بَرَكَات	blessings
125	عَبْد، عِبَاد	slave
	صَالِحِين	righteous ones

— Grammar —

255	هٰذَا	this (mg)
47	هٰذِه	this (fg)
478	ذٰلِك	that (mg)

Column 4

43	تِلْكَ	that (fg)
46	هٰؤُلَاء	these
204	أُولٰئِك	those

9: PRAYER FOR THE PROPHET

5	اَللّٰهُمَّ	O, Allah!
2	صَلِّ	Send peace!
26	ال	family, followers
	كَمَا	as
69	إِبْرَاهِيم	Ibraheem
17	حَمِيد	worthy of praise
4	مَجِيد	full of glory
	بَارِك	Send blessings
	بَارَكْت	You sent blessings

— Grammar —

only past tense 26 times

	فَعَلَ	he did
	فَعَلُوا	they all did
	فَعَلْتَ	you did
	فَعَلْتُ	I did
	فَعَلْتُمْ	you all did
	فَعَلْنَا	we did
233	جَعَلَ	he made
8	فَتَحَ	he opened

10: PRAYERS AFTER SALAH

9	اٰتِ	Give!
115	الدُّنْيَا	the world
31	حَسَنَة، حَسَنَات	good (fg)
115	الْاٰخِرَة	the hereafter (fg)
5	قِ	Protect!
322	عَذَاب	punishment
145	النَّار	the fire
	أَعِنْ	Help!
1	شُكْر	thanks
13	حُسْن	best

— Grammar —

10	نَصَرَ	he helped
150	خَلَقَ	he created
7	ذَكَرَ	he remembered
46	عَبَدَ	he worshipped

11: Surah Al-Ikhlaas (Surah No.112)

No.	Arabic	Meaning
332	قُلْ	Say!
74	أَحَد	One and only
1	اَلصَّمَد	the Self-Sufficient
348	لَمْ	did not
1	يَلِدْ ***	beget
1	يُوْلَد ***	begotten
31	يَكُنْ ***	is
1	كُفُوا	comparable
530	قَالَ ***	he said
332	قَالُوا ***	they said
106	لَنْ	will not

(Grammar)

22	ضَرَب	he hit
30	سَمِع	he listened
35	عَلِم	he Knew
99	عَمِل	he did

12: SURAH AL-FALAQ

1	اَلفَلَق ***	the daybreak
30	شَر	evil
1	غَاسِق ***	darkness
423	إِذَا	when
	وَقَب ***	becomes intense
1	اَلنَّفَّاثَت+	those who blow (fig)
4	اَلعُقَد	knots
1	حَاسِد ***	the one who envies
1	حَسَد ***	he envied
239	إِذْ	when

(Grammar) — only Imperfect tense 4 times

	يَفْعَل	he does / will do
	يَفْعَلُوْن	they do / will do
	تَفْعَل	you do / will do
	أَفْعَل	I do / will do
	تَفْعَلُوْن	you all do / will do
	نَفْعَل	we do / will do
83	يَجْعَل	he makes/ will make
2	يَفْتَح	he opens/ will open

13: SURAH AN-NAAS (Surah No.114)

13	مَلِك	King
145	إِله	God
1	اَلوَسْوَاس ***	the whisperer
44	صَدْر، صُدُوْر	chest
1	اَلخَنَّاس	the one who withdraws after whispering
1	يُوَسْوِس ***	whispers
32	اَلجِنَّة	jinn
88	مَلَك مَلَائِكَة	angel

(Grammar) — only Imperfect tense 28 times

	يَنْصُر	he helps/ will help
	يَنْصُرُوْن	they help/ will help
	تَنْصُر	you help/ will help
	أَنْصُر	I help/ will help
	تَنْصُرُوْن	you all help/ will help
	نَنْصُر	we help/ will help
23	يَخْلُق	he creates/ will create
17	يَذْكُر	he remembers/ will remember
80	يَعْبُد	he worships/ will worship

14: SURAH AL-ASR (Surah No. 103)

1	وَالعَصْر	by the time
1534	إِنَّ	indeed
65	اَلإِنْسَان	the man
2	خُسْر	loss
664	إِلَّا	except
258	آمَنُوا	they have believed
258	تَوَاصَوْا	advised each other
247	بِالحَقّ	to the truth
15	اَلصَّبْر	the patience
20	صَابِر، صَابِرُوْن، صَابِرِيْن	who are patient
691	إِنْ	if
56	شَاء	wills
280	أَوْ	or

(Grammar) — only Imperfect tense 13 times

	يَضْرِب	he hits/ will hit
	يَضْرِبُوْن	they hit/ will hit
	تَضْرِب	you hit/ will hit
	أَضْرِب	I hit/ will hit
	تَضْرِبُوْن	you all hit/ will hit
	نَضْرِب	we hit/ will hit

— only Imperfect tense 39 times

	يَسْمَع	he listens/ will listen
	يَسْمَعُوْن	they listen/ will listen
	تَسْمَع	you listen/ will listen
	أَسْمَع	I listen/ will listen
	تَسْمَعُوْن	you all listen/ will listen
	نَسْمَع	We listen/ will listen
362	يَعْلَم	he knows/ will know
166	يَعْمَل	he does/ will do
127	مَاذَا	what?

15: SURAH AN-NASR (Surah No.110)

| 171 | جَاءَ | came |
| | اَلفَتْح | the victory |

25	رَأَيْت	you saw
241	اَلنَّاس	the people
13	يَدْخُلُوْن	entering
7	فَوْج، أَفْوَاج	crowd
16	سَبِّح ***	Glorify!
10	اِسْتَغْفِر ***	Ask forgiveness!
422	كَان ***	is (was)
12	تَوَّاب، تَوَّابِيْن	one who turns often

(Grammar)

	اِفْعَل	Do!
	اِفْعَلُوا	Do! (you all)
	لَا تَفْعَل	Don't do!
	لَا تَفْعَلُوا	Don't do! (you all)

2 اِفْتَح اِفْتَحُوا لَا تَفْتَح لَا تَفْتَحُوا
22 اِجْعَل اِجْعَلُوا لَا تَجْعَل لَا تَجْعَلُوا

16: SURAH AL-KAFIROON (Surah No.109)

361	يَا	O!
153	يَاأَيُّهَا	O!
	اَعْبُد	I worship
	عَابِد عَبْدُوْن	worshipper
383	قَوْم	people

(Grammar) — only Imperfect tense 7 times

	اُنْصُر	Help!
	اُنْصُرُوا	Help! (You all)
	لَا تَنْصُر	Don't help!
	لَا تَنْصُرُوا	Don't help! (You all)

48 اُذْكُر اُذْكُرُوا لَا تَذْكُر لَا تَذْكُرُوا
37 اُعْبُد اُعْبُدُوا لَا تَعْبُد لَا تَعْبُدُوا
  اُخْلُق اُخْلُقُوا لَا تَخْلُق لَا تَخْلُقُوا

| 42 | سَوْف | soon |

17: PURPOSE OF REVELATION

261	كِتَاب، كُتُب	book
55	أَنْزَلْنَا ***	we sent down
12	مُبَارَك ***	full of blessings
1	لِيَدَّبَّرُوا ***	so that they ponder
382	آيَة، آيَات	verse
8	لِيَتَذَكَّر ***	so that (they) receive admonition
43	أُولُوا	those of
16	اَلأَلْبَاب	understanding
	بَلِّغُوا ***	Convey! (pl)
201	لَوْ	even

(Grammar)

	اِضْرِب	Hit!
	اِضْرِبُوا	Hit! (You all)
	لَا تَضْرِب	Don't hit!

	لَا تَضْرِبُوا	Don't hit! (You all)
	إِسْمَع	Listen!
	إِسْمَعُوا	Listen! (You all)
	لَا تَسْمَع	Don't listen!
	لَا تَسْمَعُوا	Don't listen (You all)

31 اِعْلَم اِعْلَمُوا لَا تَعْلَم لَا تَعْلَمُوا
11 اِعْمَل اِعْمَلُوا لَا تَعْمَل لَا تَعْمَلُوا

18: QU'RAN IS EASY TO LEARN

406	لَقَد، قَد	indeed, already
6	يَسَّرْنَا ***	We have made easy
70	اَلقُرْآن	the Qur'an
2	تَعَلَّم ***	learnt
14	عَلَّم ***	taught
145	إِنَّمَا	only
41	أَعْمَال	actions
	نِيَّات	intentions

(Grammar)

فَاعِل	مَفْعُوْل	فِعْل
doer	the one who is affected	to do
جَاعِل (6)	مَجْعُوْل	جَعْل
فَاتِح (13)	مَفْتُوْح	فَتْح
نَاصِر (35)	مَنْصُوْر	نَصْر
خَالِق (64)	مَخْلُوْق	خَلْق
ذَاكِر (79)	مَذْكُوْر	ذِكْر

19: HOW TO LEARN IT?

3	زِدْ ***	Increase!
304	اَلَّذِي	(the one) who
	قَلَم، أَقْلَام	the pen
59	أَيُّكُم	which of you
19	حَسَن	good
36	أَحْسَن	better
	عَمَلًا	deed

(Grammar)

عَابِد	مَعْبُوْد	عِبَادَة	20
ضَارِب	مَضْرُوْب	ضَرْب	3
سَامِع	مَسْمُوْع	سَمْع	22
عَالِم	مَعْلُوْم	عِلْم	134
عَامِل	مَعْمُوْل	عَمَل	42

=======================

UNDERSTAND QURAN ACADEMY

Made in the USA
Las Vegas, NV
07 November 2024

11308441R00072